# London
## STITCH & KNIT

**black dog
publishing**

london uk

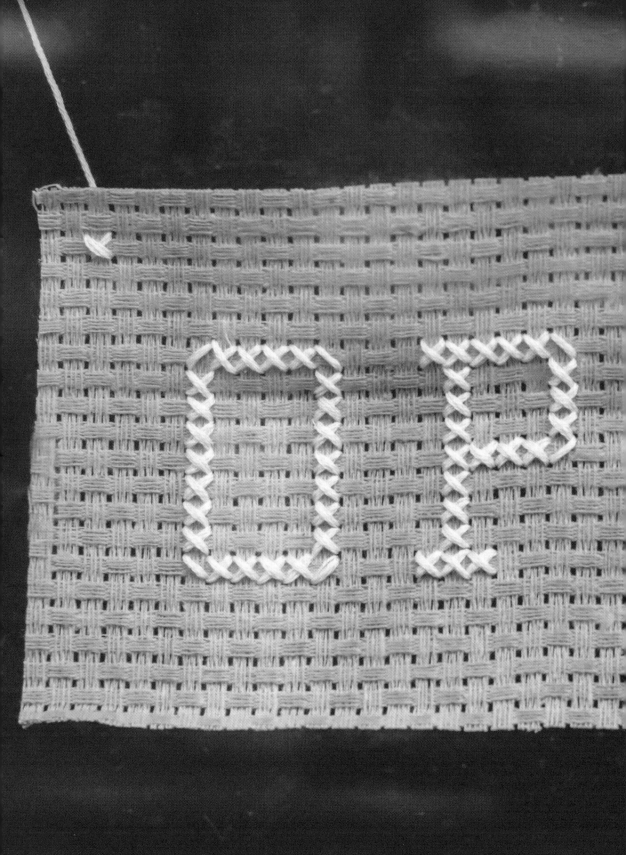

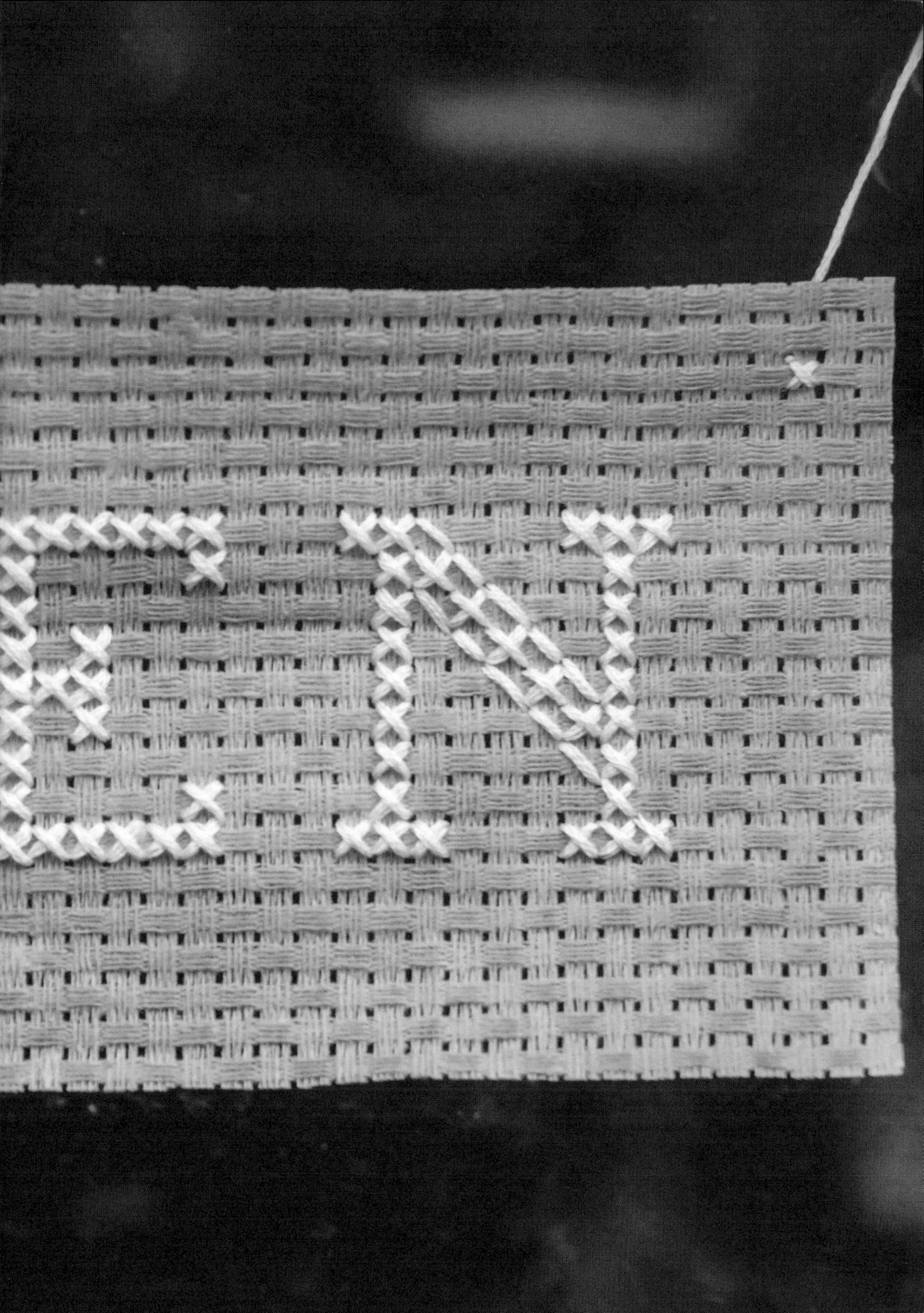

# CONTENTS

There is something quite irresistible
about a shop of crafty supplies,
a doorway into a world of possibilities;
a bundle of lace, a yard or two
of this, the inspiring colour of that,
a glue, a brown paper bag of buttons
rattling in your pocket - all of these
bring me a sense of peace knowing that
at some point along the way
they will have their moment to shine.

Rachelle Blondel

# INTRODUCTION

Make do and mend, the old Second World War adage is one we are all familiar with, one that reminds us of a time when resources were limited and people made things out of necessity. With clothing and other various household items rationed, needle and thread were diligently put to work to darn socks, repair hems and refashion any fabric scraps on hand into something useful. Waste not, want not! In the latter part of the twentieth century, though, as resources became more abundant, people were more inclined to simply buy new things rather than make use of what they had.

A throwaway attitude took hold of many, while sewing boxes collected dust. Why bother repairing that old tattered dress when you can just have a new one? But the 'more is more', 'bigger is better', 'spend, spend, spend' attitude of the 1980s and 1990s, with its various negative repercussions, eventually led people to refocus and not only start to shop more responsibly, but also see value again in making things themselves. In the last two decades, a huge shift in values has become evident as we purge ourselves of heaps of unnecessary stuff, downsize our houses, grow our own organic food, and make our own clothes and household goods again. Less out of necessity and more out of a sense of responsibility, interest and genuine pleasure, people in many respects have gone back to basics and are once again proudly picking up needle and thread.

Crafting is not simply popular now, what we are experiencing is a handmade revolution!

Craft fairs dot the globe, craft magazines line booksellers' shelves, blogs provide an unending stream of handmade inspiration, and websites such as Folksy and Etsy provide a respectable platform for independent designers to sell their wares.

When I moved to London from San Francisco in 2010, I hoped to find a few great craft supply shops. I was a beginner sewist then, but always interested in and inspired by all things handmade and by craft supplies themselves—beautiful buttons, gold thread, embroidered trimmings—I was happy to seek these things out even if I didn't actually need them for a project. Little did I know at the time the vast wealth of diverse resources this city has to offer. I scoured blogs and websites to give me clues to the best places for fabric and haberdashery supplies. Not only did I find an incredible number of wonderful shops that I now turn to, but through many of these shops, I discovered an active crafting community as well. *London Stitch and Knit* is a guide to my discoveries of the best resources for fabric, knitting and haberdashery supplies. Some of the shops in this book—such as Liberty, whose long and rich history began with imported silk fabrics—hold their own distinct and somewhat elevated place in the fabric world, while other lesser known shops—such as Simply Fabrics in Brixton, which often has bargain prices—may not have a lofty status but do have that 9-inch zip that you need. Whether you are local to London, a visiting tourist or a crafter who simply enjoys fabric, knitting and craft supplies, in this guide you can expect to find craft shops at those extremes and everything in between.

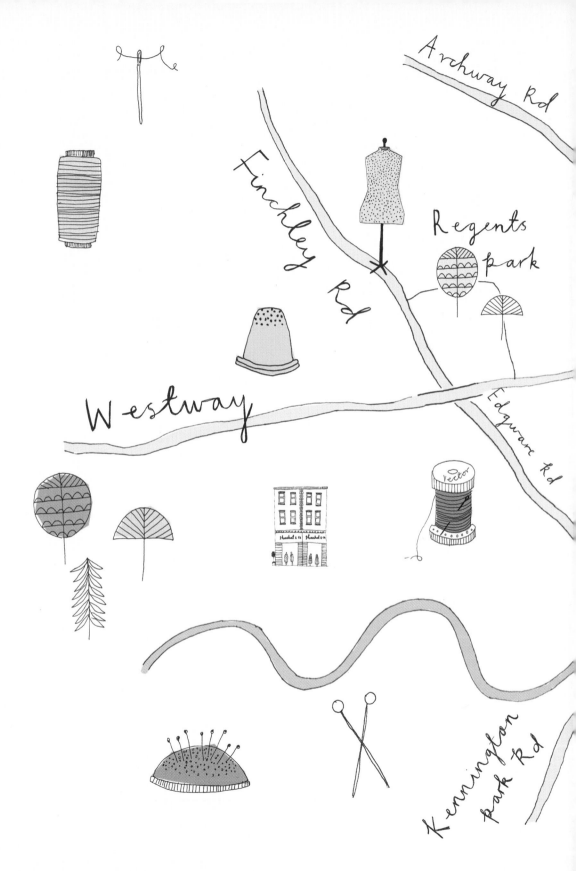

Archway Rd

Finchley Rd

Regents park

Westway

Edgware Rd

Kennington Park Rd

Kingsland Rd

thread

Victoria park

city Rd

RAY STITCH

LIBERTY

River Thames

Old kent Rd

Camberwell Rd

FABRICS

SEW OVER IT

# CENTRAL

From luxury shopping on Bond Street and centuries-old department stores such as Fortnum & Mason, to the cutting-edge design and quirky fashionable boutiques of Covent Garden, when it comes to shopping, Central London has it all. In fact, if you can't find it in Central London, it probably doesn't exist.

If you only have one day to explore the fabric and haberdashery shops of London, a good region to focus on would be around Soho, where some of the finest are concentrated. The majority of these shops are an easy hop from one another and a handful of them— Liberty, Cloth House and VV Rouleaux, for example—are simply beautiful and a pleasure to browse. The quality of merchandise and thoughtful attention to detail in these shops will leave any fabric or haberdashery lover inspired and filled with ideas to take away. Although only a few shops in this chapter have supplies for knitting and crochet, yarn lovers will be happy to wile away a few hours in the Liberty and John Lewis haberdasheries.

Shopping never fails to induce hunger, and luckily for anyone venturing to these shops, it's an area that is also brimming with the best food in the city. The nooks and crannies of Soho which surround the fabric shops on Berwick Street are populated with tempting coffee houses, cafes and restaurants. At lunchtime the scent of food wafting through restaurant doors will make your mouth water, and if you stay out late enough, you will also get a taste of the area's buzzing nightlife.

A stroll down Savile Row is a must for anybody interested in menswear or tailoring. As well as admiring the craftsmanship on display, you may catch a glimpse of the bespoke process in action through the windows of the tailors' downstairs workshops.

V V Rouleaux
Ltd

The Button
Queen

Cavendish
Square
Gardens

Oxford
Circus

John Lewis

Station

Bond
Street

Oxford Street

Station

MacCulloch
& Wallis

14

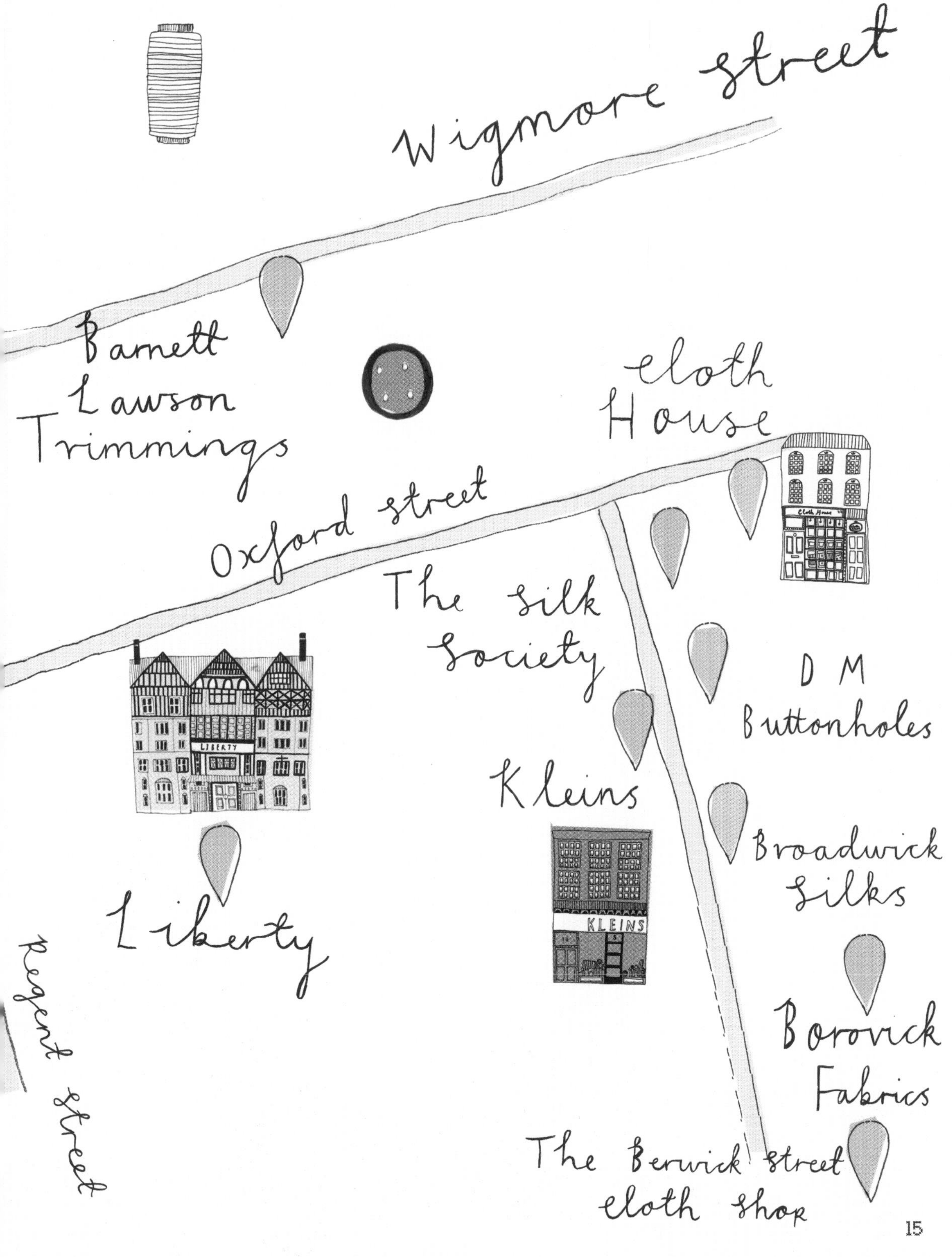

Wigmore street

Barnett
Lawson
Trimmings

Cloth
House

Oxford street

The Silk
Society

D M
Buttonholes

Kleins

Broadwick
Silks

Liberty

Borovick
Fabrics

Regent street

The Berwick street
Cloth Shop

102 Marylebone Lane
London W1U 2QD
020 7224 5179
Tube: Bond Street
www.vvrouleaux.com

# VV Rouleaux

At the north end of the lovely Marylebone Lane is VV Rouleaux, an alluring ribbon shop in a light-filled two-storey space. Annabel Lewis, a former florist, opened her first ribbon shop in 1990 and she has been inspiring designers, stylists, and milliners ever since. Her clientele ranges from established couture houses, such as Dior and Alexander McQueen, to aspiring fashion students; she has also supplied ribbons for Duchesses, Princes, and even Harry Potter.

50 colours of grosgrain, satin, organdy and wire edge ribbon in seven different widths, as well as sequined, beaded, velvet, gingham and jacquard ribbon are creatively displayed upstairs on vintage chicken feed troughs. While their selection is substantial, VV Rouleaux isn't solely a ribbon shop; interior designers take a keen interest in their range of bullion fringe and gold flanged cord, while milliners delight in their hand painted silk flowers and Lady Amherst feather mounts. Thoughtfully styled, with attention to detail at every turn, this is a shop to savour.

The VV Rouleaux headdresses on display are a testament to the superb quality of craftsmanship of their bespoke headdress service: customers are welcome to browse the shop and choose materials in consultation with a salesperson to create an original headdress. For customers eager to learn the craft themselves, VV Rouleaux offers hat and headdress courses as well as a ribbon flower course, and tassel and knot courses. *Ribbons & Trims*, Annabel Lewis' second book, which is for sale at the shop, is filled with unique ideas and instructions to customise interiors and soft furnishings with ribbons and trims.

*Wire edge ribbon (perfect for bows)*

Trimmings

11b Wardour Mews, D'arblay Street
London W1F 8AN
020 7437 8897
Tube: Oxford Circus
www.dmbuttons.co.uk

# D M Buttonholes

Soho is packet with little hidden gems, and one for costumiers, tailors and dressmakers is nestled underground on Wardour Mews. While it may be a bit of a speciality shop, anyone who fears wrecking a garment with wonky buttonholes after spending hours, possibly even days or weeks, making it will be relieved to know they can have them done professionally for just a few pounds. DM Buttonholes is a family business that has been in operation for nearly 100 years. In his basement workspace, David Miller sews buttonholes on garments for fashion students, costume designers, tailors, seamstresses and home sewers. He has done buttonholes on clothing for celebrities including Princess Diana and Angelina Jolie, as well as for a multitude of costumes in film and TV, including the 2015 Kenneth Branagh production of *Cinderella* and popular period drama *Downton Abbey*.

David's basement shop is dotted with vintage buttonhole sewing machines which he uses because "they're simply better than their modern counterparts". He offers a variety of buttonhole styles: straight, keyhole and lapel buttonholes to name a few. In addition to the buttonhole service, he also offers covered button and covered cufflink services, and can rivet or grommet practically any fabric by request. There's no need to make an appointment either, as David is happy to fulfil customers' requests while they wait.

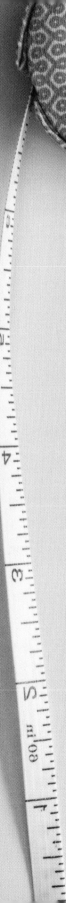

300 Oxford St
London W1C 1DX
020 7629 7711
Tube: Oxford Circus
www.johnlewis.com

# John Lewis

Quintessential British department store John Lewis has everything you would expect: clothing, housewares and electronics. Their Oxford Street branch also happens to feature an admirable haberdashery department with many lovely fabrics for patchwork, dressmaking and some for home furnishings; a good selection of sewing patterns; a wide variety of haberdashery supplies and sewing machines; pretty ribbons and trimmings—many of which are by VV Rouleaux; and some great sewing, knitting and needlework craft kits.

A playful tone is expressed in many of John Lewis' haberdashery products, as in their own range of candy-coloured sewing machines in shades that range from "dusky pink" to "spearmint green". The John Lewis line of sewing and knitting baskets and accessories are equally cheerful in a variety of great prints and patterns. Cute craft kits are offered for adults and children alike; mini-felt friends and sock creature kits for children, knicker and tie kits for adults.

The focal point of the haberdashery is "The Makery"—a workspace for courses offered in-store in partnership with The Makery shop in Bath. These courses are primarily designed for beginners. Sewing a clasp purse, sewing a cushion cover, making your own bias binding, and making your own espadrilles are a few of the courses offered.

If you are local to London and interested in purchasing a sewing machine at a John Lewis store, not only do their range of machines have great reviews but they also offer a free lesson on how to use your machine when you're ready to start sewing.

Quality No: Z181
Colour: Ivory
Price per Metre:

25–26 Poland Street
London W1F 8QN
020 7629 0311
Tube: Oxford Circus
www.macculloch-wallis.co.uk

# MacCulloch & Wallis

Formerly housed on Dering Street in a traditional shop that looked as though it hadn't changed a bit since Victorian times, MacCullouch & Wallis moved to a new, modern space on Poland Street in spring 2015. Merchandise that used to be spread over five small floors is now spread over two larger ones. MacCulloch & Wallis is easily a one-stop shop. Fabrics of a multitude of prints and materials are stacked on shelves or neatly hang from racks on hangers. These sample racks are an ingenious idea, making it very easy for customers to not only see and feel the fabrics, but to take a sample just by snipping off a small piece. With this system in place, there is no need to mess about pulling rolls off high shelves or worrying about a pile of fabric toppling over.

Lovely fabrics aside, MacCullouch & Wallis also have practically any haberdashery item one could possibly think of, from beautiful trims—including leather, beaded and feathered—to specialised items for garment construction, such as corset and lingerie accessories and millinery supplies, to a plethora of industrial or domestic machine needles and hand sewing needles that combined form a collection of needles bigger than you are ever likely to see again. If you are searching for swimwear accessories or reflective trim, MacCulloch & Wallis have that too.

The salespeople are very knowledgeable, friendly and happy to help with any query. And if you can think of anything MacCullouch & Wallis is missing, they welcome suggestions for new supplies and materials.

DARNERS SIZE 7

DARNERS SIZE 5

CHENILLE SIZE 22

25 N

DARNERS SIZE 3

PESTRY 22

CH SIZE

STRY

PRICE

COTTON DARNERS

PESTRY

PRICE
£45.60

WOMEN'S WEAR BASIC TROUSER BLOCK

SIZES 10-22 • NO SEAM ALLOWANCES ADDED

WOMEN'S WEAR BASIC TROUSER BLOCK

SIZES 10-22
NO SEAM
ALLOWANCES ADDED

WOMEN'S WEAR BASIC

'S WEAR BAS

BRA
STRAPS

BRA
FASTENERS

BRA
UNDERWI

CORSET
LACES 3m

CORSET
LACES 4m

CORSE
LACES 5

Regent Street
London W1B 5AH
020 7734 1234
Tube: Oxford Circus
www.liberty.co.uk

# Liberty

**L**ondoners likely need no introduction to Liberty, but for readers unfamiliar with this iconic department store, it produces some of the finest fabric in the world. Liberty's lengthy history started with its conception by Arthur Liberty in 1875, in its first guise as East India House on Regent Street. Customers were enthralled by the textiles, furniture and art imported from Japan, China and India, in which the shop specialised. As popularity in the merchandise grew, so did the store and in 1924, during a fashionable Tudor revival, Liberty commissioned the construction of a mock Tudor building on Great Marlborough Street. Constructed of timbers from two ships, the HMS Impregnable and HMS Hindustan, the stunning Tudor-style building still stands today and is a striking beauty in an otherwise modern concrete shopping mecca.

To admire the building is reason enough to visit Liberty, but what will keep you there are the individual departments filled with exquisite products—the haberdashery and fabric department being one of the most popular. Liberty classic Tana Lawn fabric, named so from Lake Tana in East Africa, where the cotton was originally produced, is a lightweight 100 per cent cotton that is ideal for dressmaking. In addition to the classic Tana Lawn prints in ditsy floral, paisley and abstract designs, Liberty produces seasonal Liberty Art Fabrics centred around a theme and designed by various artists, such as the 2015 Alice in Wonderland collection exploring Alice's adventures. While the majority of Liberty fabric is Tana Lawn, they also sell their prints in a number of other materials including jersey, georgette and corduroy. Knitters will also take a great interest in Liberty's range of yarns, books and patterns for knitting and crochet. The Liberty Sewing School offers Saturday courses in sewing, knitting and crochet, and afternoon tea is provided with the courses.

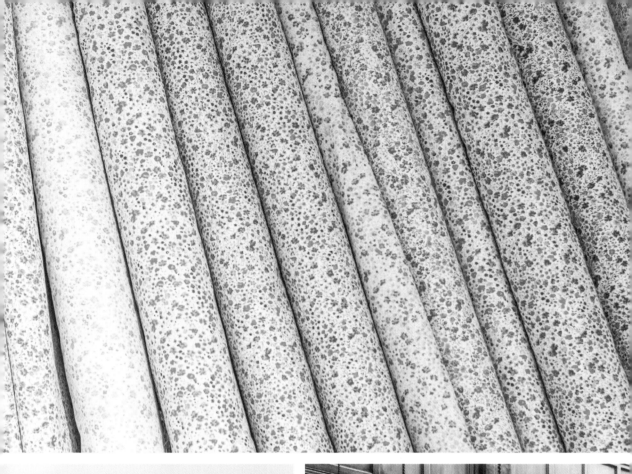

16–17 Little Portland Street
London W1W 8NE
020 7636 8591
Tube: Oxford Circus
www.bltrimmings.com

# Barnett Lawson trimmings

To theatre costumiers and fashion designers in the know, Barnett Lawson Trimmings is a tremendous resource. But for those not already acquainted, it's a treasure trove awaiting discovery. There is no storefront, only a plain metal door with a buzzer. Upon entering, customers make their way along a hallway and then through another door, which leads into a basement wonderland of trimmings. It has an air of exclusivity, but for half a century Barnett Lawson Trimmings has sold not only to the trade but to the general public as well. Their clientele ranges from famous fashion designers and celebrity stylists, who still visit in person, to the home dressmaker and amateur milliner. Owner Caroline Marx says their motto is: "If we don't stock it, we can source it." She relishes the challenge of sourcing supplies from their vast database of suppliers.

With shelves filled to the ceiling with boxes of trimmings, it is almost hard to believe there is anything a customer would want that she wouldn't have. They sell over 12,000 different items, including double-faced satin ribbon, frogging, elastics, decorative butterflies and birds, sequin trims, feathers, paper flowers, fancy buttons, cords, tassels and millinery supplies, to name just a few! They can also custom dye feathers and trims, make bespoke corsages and print personalised ribbons, as well as provide free samples by scan or post. Although their merchandise is clearly identifiable, labelled and priced, the knowledgeable staff are happy to help customers with any queries.

Vintage Glass Button's 50p each

47 Berwick Street
London W1F 8SJ
020 7437 5155
Tube: Oxford Circus
www.clothhouse.com

# cloth House

**N**iki and Jay Harley started Cloth House 30 years ago with the desire to create a textile store where they supplied to the public all the fabrics they loved but often couldn't find. Niki says, "from this initial idea, every roll of cloth has been selected by us on its merits alone and not merely to fill a shelf". With an emphasis on natural fibres, Niki and Jay are passionate about sourcing materials directly from artisans and local textile traders to ensure both the materials' quality and to support the local artisans themselves and their economies. Formerly with two stores on Berwick Street until spring 2015, the two shops have now merged to the one at 47 Berwick Street.

The remarkable range of fabrics at Cloth House include lightweight cottons such as poplin and heavyweight cottons such as denim and canvas; linens such as painted linen and shirting linen; and technical fabrics such a neoprene, latex and foil ripstop. Cloth House also has a beautiful selection of wool, felt, cashmere, silk, lace, velvet and jersey fabric, to name a few. These are not fabrics you will want use for your first sewing lesson—Cloth House is the sort of shop to go to when you want to make something special out material that is equally exceptional. The shop is also a wonderful resource for lovely sewing accessories such as Indian tailors' scissors and a range of vintage haberdashery, including vintage buttons, trims and thread.

The decor of the shop is as inspiring as the merchandise. Among the fabrics are framed oil paintings, collections of vintage needlework books, and vintage haberdashery creatively displayed stacked inside wooden crates, all of which add to the shop's timeless, welcoming atmosphere.

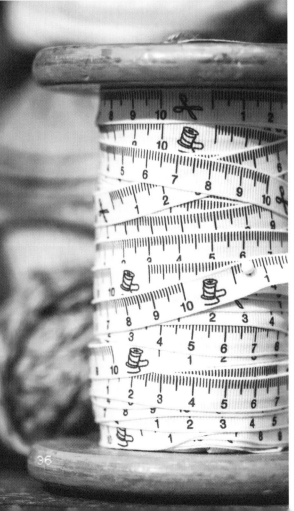

Please use this tray for buttons.

Please use this tray for buttons.

Please use this tray for buttons.

9–11 Broadwick Street
London W1F 0DB
020 7734 3320
Tube: Oxford Circus
www.broadwicksilks.com

# Broadwick Silks

Spencer Harvey and Michael Greene opened Broadwick Silks in 1990 with the goal of creating a shop that sold fine fabrics, catering to fabric buyers from the film, theatre and couture fashion industry, as well as the general sewing public. The shop is one of three owned by Spencer and Michael, all of which are within a short walk of each other in the centre of London's dynamic West End, a perfect location for costumiers, dressmakers, tailors and fashion students to source materials.

Broadwick Silks—the first of the three shops to open—has a brilliant range of silks in a multitude of colours and variations. Embroidered silks, chiffons, velvets, beaded laces and brocades are a few of the luxury fabrics customers will find on the shelves. The largest of their three stores, The Berwick Street Cloth Shop at 14 Berwick Street, which opened in 1994, has a more eccentric selection of fabrics including fur, leather, PVC, denim, wool, polyester, cotton and plain silks. Their third shop, The Silk Society at 44 Berwick Street, opened in 1995 and sells some of their most exquisite fabrics which are in high demand from their couture fashion clientele.

Close to 80 per cent of the fabrics for sale at Broadwick Silks and its sister-stores are made specially and many have had their moment to shine—Spencer and Michael's shops are credited as suppliers of costume fabrics for numerous West End productions including *Les Miserables*, *Cats* and *Wicked*, and films including *Titanic*, *Pirates of the Caribbean* and *The Lord of the Rings*.

5 Noel Street
London W1F 8GD
020 7437 6162
Tube: Oxford Circus
www.kleins.co.uk

# kleins

Among the concentration of fabric shops in Soho is one haberdashery that will fill any crafter's toolbox to the brim. Mary Klein opened Kleins in 1936, selling sewing thread and offering a covered button service. Her husband, Alfred, later joined her in running the business and over the next 50 years they together built Kleins, which is now owned and run by their grandson, Raymond Bryer.

The shop's exterior deceivingly gives the impression of a miniature space; the more muted and monotone colours of the haberdashery supplies in the small upstairs room are sharply contrasted with the world of colour one encounters in the shop's sizeable downstairs. Upstairs customers will find basics such as pins, needles, dyes, clasps, various fasteners and zips. Downstairs is a rainbow of ribbon, thread, trims and cording. Kleins has a great reputation for their unusual zip fasteners and specialist interfacings as well as their Japanese trimmings by Mokuba, which Raymond says "are a must for any trimming enthusiast".

All of the staff at Kleins have a background in sewing or fashion and are knowledgeable about the products they sell and how to use them, providing the best advice to customers. Raymond says "we don't just sell them the product and wish them a good day. I want to make sure the person buying it knows how to [use it] or apply it and get the best possible use out of it."

16 Berwick Street
London W1F 0HP
020 7437 2180
Tube: Oxford Circus
www.borovickfabrics.com

# Borovick Fabrics

One of the more modest looking fabric shops on Berwick Street is Borovick Fabrics. With its simple grey and black facade and rolls of fabrics leaning on the entryway, this is one fabric shop whose unassuming appearance contrasts with its exceptional stock. Established in 1932, Borovick is a family-run business and the oldest fabric store in Soho. Costume designers, fashion designers, fashion students and home sewers alike turn to Borovick Fabrics for a diverse range of high quality fabrics.

Much of the stock at the front of the store is eye-catchingly glitzy—shimmery sequined fabric, glossy tinted PVC, and brightly coloured fluffy feather boas command attention. Adjoining rooms contain a huge range of fabrics including jersey, chiffon, crepe, satin, dupion and georgette, to name a few. Their bridal range includes lace, brocade and silk, and they have a variety of suiting fabrics many of which are made by Dormeuil.

But, as director Simon Lipman puts it, "Borovick is so much more than just the fabrics you see". Their great reputation with manufacturers and loyal relationships with customers may not be readily apparent but make Borovick Fabrics well known and trusted in the industry. Their commitment to excellent customer service doesn't stop at the door; for customers who may not be able to make it into the shop, Borovick Fabrics offer a worldwide free sample swatch service.

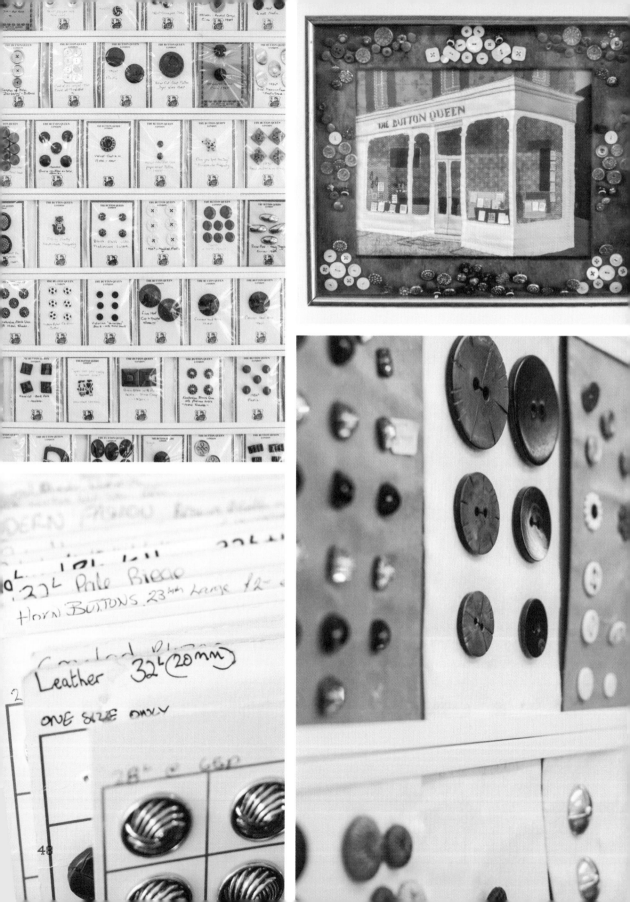

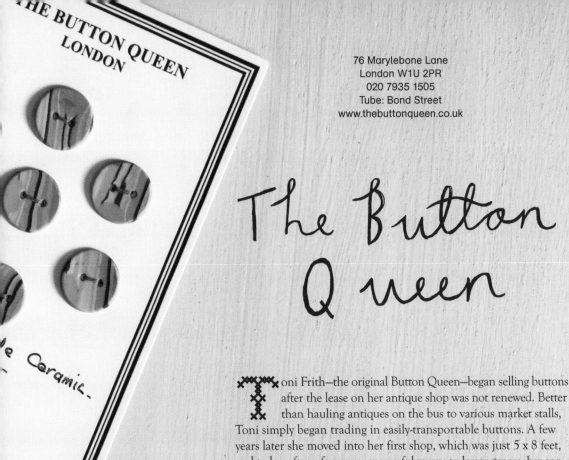

76 Marylebone Lane
London W1U 2PR
020 7935 1505
Tube: Bond Street
www.thebuttonqueen.co.uk

# The Button Queen

**T**oni Frith—the original Button Queen—began selling buttons after the lease on her antique shop was not renewed. Better than hauling antiques on the bus to various market stalls, Toni simply began trading in easily-transportable buttons. A few years later she moved into her first shop, which was just 5 x 8 feet, and today, after a few more successful moves to larger spaces, her son Martyn Frith runs The Button Queen on Marylebone Lane.

The simple and somewhat sparse interior with white walls and wood flooring only serves as a backdrop to highlight rows of buttons on blue and white button cards. Though there are hundreds of buttons displayed on the walls, it would be impossible to display everything The Button Queen has in stock so Martyn has numerous button card books categorised by material, such as horn or leather, with numbers that correspond with numerous button trays in the back room. After a customer chooses a desired button, he retrieves it in size and quantity from the back. Curious customers at The Button Queen will find modern, vintage and antique buttons that range from a few pence to hundreds of pounds, in materials as diverse as wood, leather, metal, plastic, glass, and pearl, to name just a few!

Whether you are looking for a few unassuming plastic buttons for a standard shirt, a large, one-off art deco button for a vintage cape, or period-perfect buttons for a *Macbeth* production costume, simply anyone in need of a button will find the perfect piece at The Button Queen.

A bag of beautiful buttons is the grown-up version of a bag of sweets.

Both require careful choosing which should be savoured, not rushed.

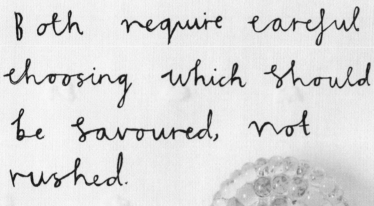

Jane Brocket

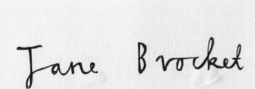

CSN6

Embroidery
Size 5/10

WILLIAMS

16 Needles

# NORTH

From picturesque Hampstead, and elegant Primrose Hill, to characterful Camden Town, North London is brimming with charming neighbourhoods, beautiful parks, terrific shops and an often-lovely hilly terrain that provides vantage points from which to admire the scenery. With so much to offer, it is easy to see why North Londoners have such pride of place. Neighbourhoods like Islington and Marylebone are great for a stroll and excellent options for shopping and dining, while the parks in North London cannot be beaten. Regent's Park, for example, with mature and meticulously manicured gardens, inviting deck chairs that dot the lawns for public use, a waterfall, boating lake, open-air theatre, and London Zoo, is a quintessential London park that locals are lucky to have on their doorstep.

While the shops in this chapter are quite a distance from each other, North London has a great variety of everything for textile and fibre lovers—with speciality shops selling materials from buttons to leather, and supplies for not only sewing and knitting, but also specifically for weaving and embroidery as well. In addition to the shops featured here, one hotspot for knit fabrics is Cannon Street Jersey Fabrics who manufacture their own fabrics on the premises and offer jersey fabric at unbeatable prices.

A number of the shops in this chapter offer courses, but for anyone keen to do more sewing than shopping, The Thrifty Stitcher in Stoke Newington, run by Claire-Louise Hardie, Author of *The Great British Sewing Bee: Fashion with Fabric*, is an excellent sewing school, and Little Hands Designs in Belsize Park is another sewing school with a focus on courses for kids and teens.

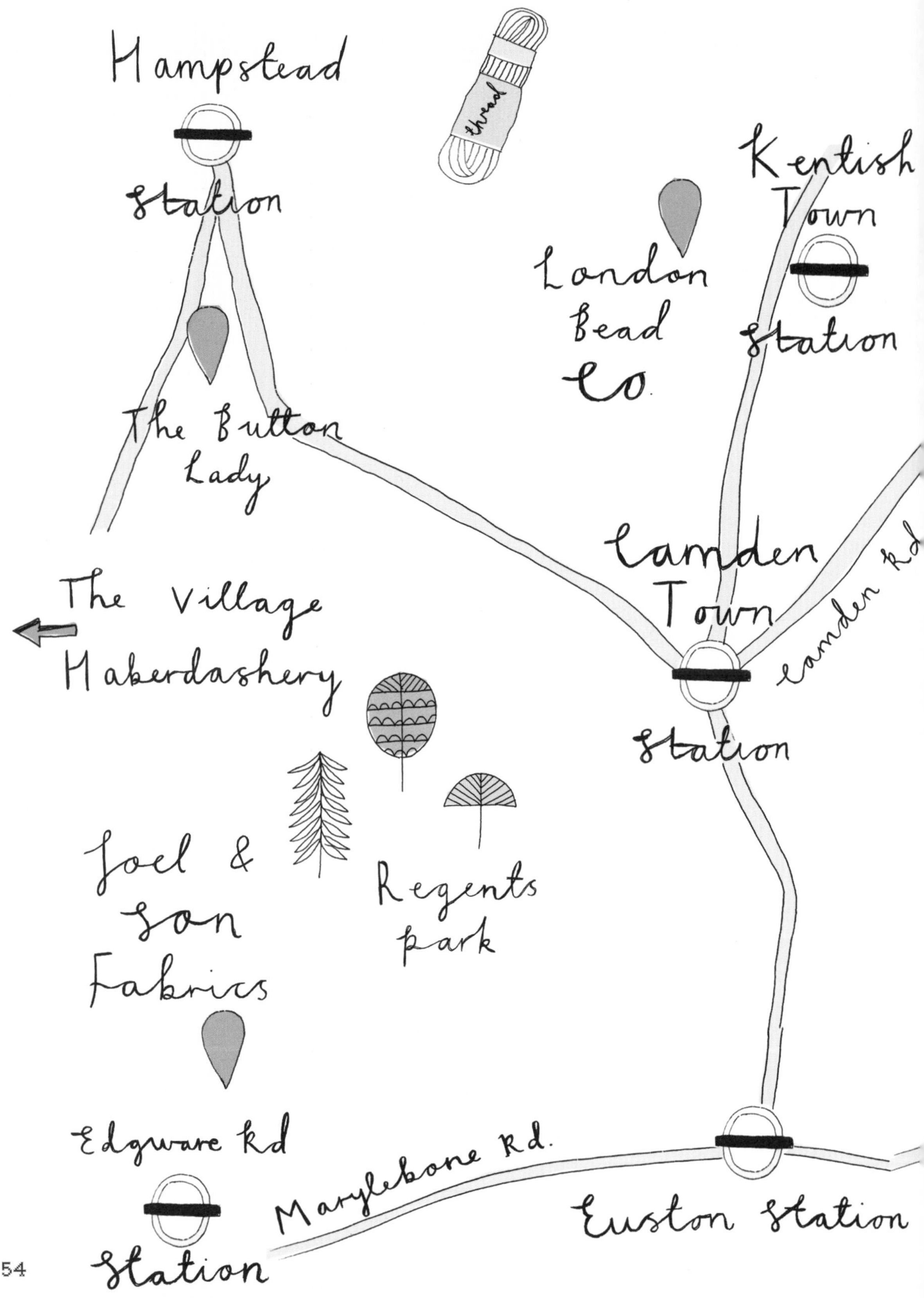

Hampstead

Station

The Button
Lady

The Village
Haberdashery

←

Joel &
Son
Fabrics

Edgware Rd

Station

Marylebone Rd.

Regents
park

thread

London
Bead
Co.

Kentish
Town

Station

Camden
Town

camden Rd

Station

Euston station

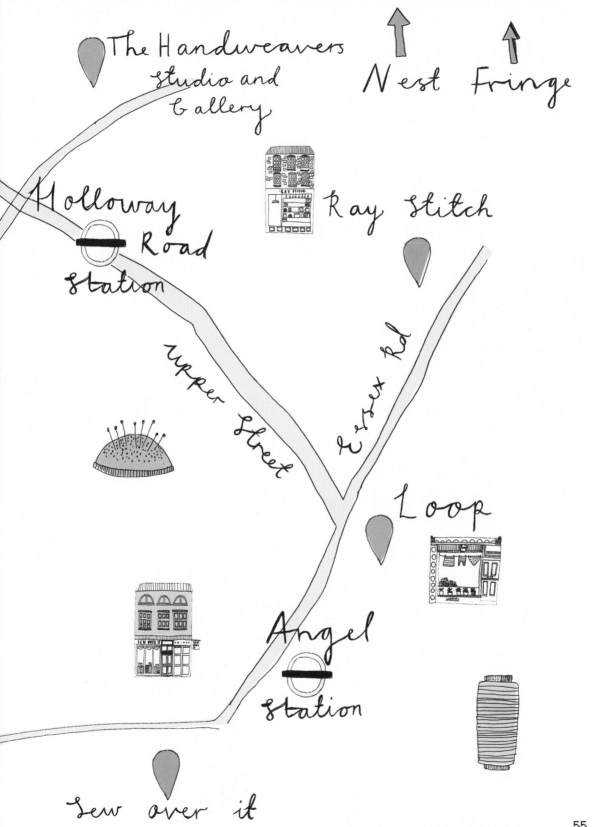

The Handweavers Studio and Gallery

Nest Fringe

Ray Stitch

Holloway Road Station

Upper Street

Essex Rd

Loop

Angel Station

Sew over it

55

SEW OVER IT

Betty Dress

56

CUSTOMISING *JAR*

CUSTOMISING *JAR*

CUSTOMISING *JAR*

36A Myddelton Street
London EC1R 1UA
020 7326 0376
Tube: Angel
www.sewoverit.co.uk

# Sew over it

The second Sew Over It location, which opened in Islington in 2014, is sister-store to owner Lisa Comfort's other Clapham branch. While it may be a bit smaller and the purple and blue colour scheme digresses from the signature hot pink and blue of the original store, Sew Over It's Islington location is just as welcoming and offers a comfortable space for taking sewing courses. Sew Over It in Islington sells many of the same terrific fabrics and haberdashery supplies—many of which Lisa sources herself on her travels to locations as exotic as India—as well as their popular range of original patterns and project kits, which make great gifts. And, just as at Sew Over It in Clapham, the Islington branch's customers can take part in courses including numerous dressmaking classes, and will find for sale Lisa's popular books—the latest being *Sew Over It Vintage*, which covers 30 sewing projects and customising ideas to create vintage inspired clothing and housewares.

In addition to the Sew Over It blog, where you will find "sewalong" posts in multiple segments covering how to make a Sew Over It pattern from start to finish, Lisa has a number of informative videos on YouTube, such as how to insert a concealed zip and attach facing to a neckline. But if you need help in person, Sew Over It's sewing cafe is a wonderful space where anyone can hire time to work on a sewing machine, or simply seek help with a project.

102 Weston Park
London N8 9PP
020 8340 8852
Tube: Finsbury Park
National rail: Harringay
www.nestknitting.com

# Nest

Formerly one of Nest's loyal customers, Genevieve West took over the shop in 2015 when the original owner moved abroad. A comfortable space with a wool shop at the front and an area for courses at the rear, Nest is a spot customers find "warm and welcoming without being twee", according to Genevieve. The shop largely focuses on knitting—stocking a generous supply of yarn, brands of which include Woolyknits, Erika Knight, Debbi Bliss and their own brand, Nest Naturals—but sells a selection of lovely fabric and offers sewing courses as well.

Having spent two years running the sewing school at Ray Stitch in partnership with Ray Stitch owner, Rachel Hart, Genevieve was eager to establish sewing courses at Nest and now, in addition to adult dressmaking courses, Nest welcomes little sewists with a range of sewing courses for young children and teens. To support the sewing classes, Genevieve sells haberdashery supplies as well as patterns from independent pattern designers such as Gather, Little Woollie and Maker's Atelier.

At the centre of the shop is a pleasant seating area and the popular Nest lending library; customers can borrow two books at a time for up to 20 days, a perfect amount of time to get inspired and complete a project from one of the many great craft books on display.

'Last Chance' Buttons

47 Mill Lane
London NW6 1NB
020 7794 5635
Tube: West Hampstead
www.thevillagehaberdashery.co.uk

# The Village Haberdashery

Beautiful modern, colourful fabrics are what stand out most at The Village Haberdashery. If you enjoy any patchwork crafts such as quilting, or if you are a dressmaker who loves contemporary prints by current designers, The Village Haberdashery will have your sewing room fabric stash overflowing in no time. A rainbow of fabrics lines the tall shelves of The Village Haberdashery, with prints from designers such as Leah Duncan, Bonnie Christine and Elizabeth Olwen. In addition to an incredible selection of cotton prints, plentiful other fabrics, such as jersey and interlock knits in a multitude of solids and stripes are on offer.

While fabric makes up the majority of their stock, The Village Haberdashery also has a lovely range of yarns from companies such as MillaMia and UK Alpaca as well as a great selection of haberdashery for sewing, knitting, crochet and embroidery. Owner Annie Barker says that The Village Haberdashery is, "especially fond of products that offer a modern spin on traditional craft". One such example are Jenny Hart's Sublime Stitching embroidery patterns, with motifs including unicorns and robots.

Most of the products on sale at The Village Haberdashery are also available on their website, as are subscriptions to their very own "Village Stash Society" which features a baby quilt club and a colour of the month club. Classes at The Village Haberdashery include a variety of quilting, dressmaking, knitting and crochet courses. For children, there are after school sewing and knitting clubs too, and their blog, The Daily Stitch, is regularly updated with posts about new products, events and free patterns and tutorials.

learn to sew! learn to knit

ask for a

# CLASS SCHEDULE

quilting • dressmaking • embroidery • crochet
knitting • appliqué • home furnishings • cross stitch
children's classes • parties • machine rental
and more!

MIXED ART DECO

HAND MADE
GLASS BUTTONS C.1955

202 £15
201 £15
204 £20
205 £15
208 £12
207

12 Heath Street
London NW3 6TE
020 7435 5412
Tube: Hampstead
www.the-button-lady.hostedbywebstore.co.uk

# The Button Lady

**H**ampstead, a quaint village-like neighbourhood with rolling hills and narrow winding streets, is almost postcard-perfect in its charming appearance. Somewhat obscured behind a gate on Heath Street is a gem in this village, a delightful brick courtyard lane, home of the Hampstead Antiques Emporium where Phyllis Caras, "The Button Lady", has been selling buttons for more than 20 years. Her initial introduction to buttons came from her parents and grandparents who were in the garment manufacturing business. While trading antiques, she received so many compliments on the buttons on her blouses, and possessed such an ever-growing personal button collection that she began to sell them alongside her antiques. Such a hit were the buttons that she eventually began to sell them almost exclusively and soon acquired her moniker.

This petite shop is so small one can barely turn around in it, but it's room enough for Phyllis and her thousands of buttons: handmade glass, hand painted porcelain, bakelite, horn, and metal buttons from various periods overflow in the tiny shop. The majority of the buttons are in drawers and displayed on button cards or loose in trays. While they may not be displayed in the most organised fashion, Phyllis is happy to let customers have a rummage through the colour sorted drawers and trays, and if you have a specific request, she knows just where to look for it. During slow times along the lane she offers the other antiques traders the chance to sort buttons. "How can anyone be bored looking at buttons?" she says with a big smile.

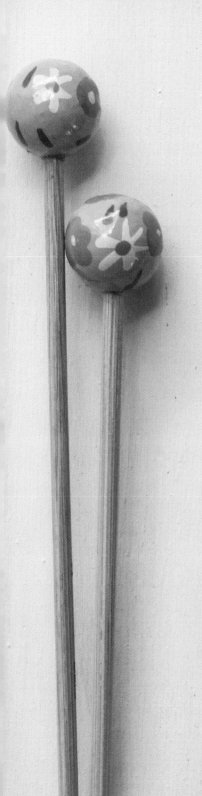

108 Alexandra Park Road
London N10 2AE
020 8883 9478
Tube: Bounds Green
National Rail: Alexandra Palace
www.fringe108.london

# Fringe

Just a short stroll from Alexandra Park is Fringe, one of a handful of excellent shops on Alexandra Park Road in Muswell Hill. Judith Isherwood, architect and craft enthusiast, opened Fringe in 2011. Combining her skills as an architect along with her passion for textile crafts, Judith converted an old betting shop into a stunning space that serves as a shop, gallery and classroom. High ceilings, exposed brick walls and lovely wood farm tables give the shop a warm and welcoming atmosphere—the perfect environment for shopping for handmade gifts and taking creative workshops.

Judith's affection for independent design reveals itself in the terrific selection of handmade items she sells. British design is fundamental to her philosophy and she tries to support the work of UK-based designer-makers in her range of products, which also have a focus on natural materials. From Jayne Middlebrook's intricate lace jewellery to Joan O'Hanlon's hand-knit children's cardigans, the display tables and cases at Fringe are thoughtfully displayed will all manner of beautiful handmade designs. "With so much to browse and inspire it's easy to while away an hour and leave with a treasure you may not have seen before", Judith says.

In addition to these delightful handmade items, Fringe is brimming with yarn, fabrics and haberdashery supplies, including a selection of vintage pieces, such as genuine Vogue sewing patterns. Customers will also find a variety of fun DIY packs, such as Hawthorn felt animal kits. Fringe offer all of the supplies needed to take one of their sewing, knitting or crochet courses, as well as offering one-on-one sessions to help customers progress their skills. Judith says this specialised attention "enables customers to complete their project and leave us with the confidence to conquer their next one".

339 Kentish Town Road
London NW5 2TJ
020 7267 9403
Tube: Kentish Town
www.londonbeadco.co.uk

# London Bead co

Following in her mother's and grandmother's footsteps, in the early 1980s owner Faye Niven took her passion for crafting and opened a shop in Fremantle, Western Australia where she sold general craft and patchwork supplies. As the business grew the range increased to include embroidery, smocking and heirloom sewing supplies. Faye's daughter, Alexandra Kidd—a bead enthusiast—later joined the business and in 1991 they made the move from Australia to London to set up shop here too. The London Bead Company now sells the largest range of hand embroidery threads and Swarovski crystals in the country.

Conveniently located just across from Kentish Town underground station, The London Bead Company is likely to impress any needlecrafter or jewellery designer with its radiant and diverse array of shimmery merchandise. The long shop consists of two fairly narrow, joined rooms that are equally brimming with a rainbow of delicate supplies. One entire wall is lined with Miyuki Seed and Delica beads, and the glass display case in the centre of the shop provides a clear view of their selection of glittering Swarovski crystals, which are available as sew-on stones, bi-cone beads and fancier cuts, such as diamond shapes. In the back of the shop is a brilliant display of classic DCM embroidery thread on one wall and a large selection of other embroidery threads such as hand-dyed Gumnut Yarns and Kacoonda silk, wool and mohair threads.

73

76

73 Church Street
London NW8 8EU
020 7724 6895
Tube: Edgeware Road
www.joelandsonfabrics.com

# Joel & Son Fabrics

Not every shop can say they have a Royal Warrant from the Queen, but Joel & Son Fabrics is one that can. This royal seal of approval which recognises organisations that supply goods to the monarchy is awarded to Joel & Son Fabrics as their fabrics can often be spotted being worn by the Queen. As one might imagine, fabrics worthy of this honour happen to have a price tag to match—many fabrics at Joel & Son are well into three digits per metre, the majority of which are luxury pieces made in Italy and France. Cashmere, lace, brocade and jacquard are just a few of the fine fabrics on offer here, and many of these are designer brands from the likes of Versace and Armani. They also carry some Swarovski brand fabrics and trimmings adorned, of course, with Swarovski crystals.

Walking into Joel & Son Fabrics for the first time, you will likely be stunned by the quantity of fabrics on show. The shop is enormous; fabrics in stacks and rolls to the ceiling are calling out for attention with their white information tags which flap about like confetti in a breeze. Even if you find visible price tags unsightly, there is something to be said for a shop that clearly marks each item with its material, origin, price and item number.

The staff are charming and helpful, and while their fabrics might have a grand status, the salespeople are down to earth. On the shop's website there is an informative A–Z glossary of fabrics, which any enthusiast will find a pleasure to dip into.

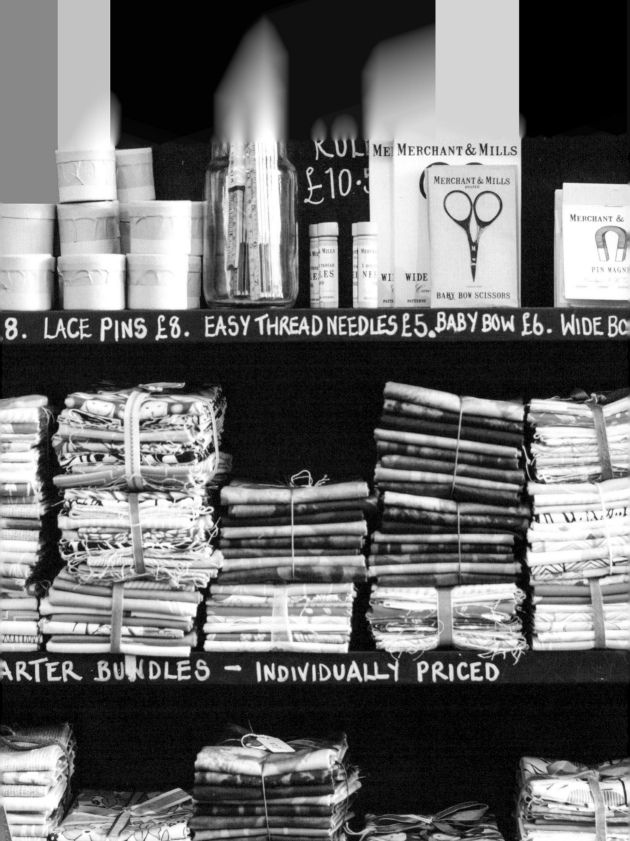

99 Essex Road
London N1 2SJ
020 7704 1060
National Rail: Essex Road
www.raystitch.co.uk

# Ray Stitch

Just a few blocks north of Islington Green on Essex Road is Ray Stitch, a one stop haberdashery and sewing school. Rachel Hart, owner of Ray Stitch, started her shop online in 2008 and opened the Islington storefront in 2011. Upstairs is the shop, which features rows of beautiful modern fabrics, books, patterns and a carefully chosen selection of haberdashery supplies. Downstairs is the sewing room, which features a long communal sewing table that provides plenty of space for classes.

Rachel offers customers an inspirational experience to buy everything for a project in one place. She says she "really wants people to feel the excitement of planning a unique and original garment". From pattern to fabric to buttons to trims, the friendly staff at Ray Stitch are happy to help customers choose everything needed to see their work through to the end. They sell an extensive selection of patterns by indie pattern companies such as Named Clothing and Papercut, as well as lovely fabrics by companies including Birch Organics, Kokka and Cotton + Steele.

Some of Ray Stitch's sewing courses include an introduction to machine sewing, sewing children's clothes, dressmaking, patchwork and quilting, but the pattern cutting classes are their speciality. Finding that people often have trouble fitting commercial patterns to themselves—getting the fit right for your own particular body can be tricky—Rachel created the pattern cutting classes, in which students learn to create their own pattern block to avoid any commercial pattern fitting issues in the future.

Ribbon 70p per Metre ↓    Ribbon 70p per

COTTON TAPE

PLEASE FEEL FREE
TO USE THE iPAD TO
BROWSE OUR CLASSES,
OUR RANGE OF PATTERNS
AND ALL THE LATEST

INDEPENDENCE TRAIL WOOL  138CM WIDE    £23/m    100% BOILED WOOL  144CM WIDE    £23/m    BRODY WEAVE WOOL BLEND  154CM WI

140 Seven Sisters Road
London N7 7NS
020 7272 1891
Tube: Arsenal
National Rail: Finsbury Park
www.handweavers.co.uk

# The Handweavers Studio & Gallery

**W**eavers, knitters and embroiderers will find themselves in fibre heaven at the The Handweavers Studio & Gallery. Formerly located in Walthamstow, where it opened 40 years ago, The Handweavers Studio & Gallery moved to Finsbury Park in 2009, where they now occupy a sizable shop, filled with neatly organised shelves that display a tremendous selection of yarn, fibres, equipment, tools, dyes and books. Alongside yarns made from standard materials such as wool, rayon and silk, customers will find a number of somewhat more unusual ones, such as fine overtwisted yarns for special collapse effects in weaving and knitting, as well as a range of paper yarns and yarns that incorporate wire. Their fibre range includes merino, wool, silk and many plant fibres and hair fibres such as fine soya tops and even camel down. In addition to weaving looms and spinning wheels, The Handweavers Studio & Gallery is one of the few places you can buy tassel moulds and small tools such as gripfids.

Beautiful samples are on display throughout the shop, giving customers an idea of the various ways in which their yarns and fibres can be used. Looms are also set up for customers to try out and several short courses in weaving and spinning—as well as a two-year part-time diploma in weaving—are on offer. Many of The Handweavers Studio & Gallery's products are available online and offered in amounts as small as 25gms.

paper + raw silk

8.8 nm
8,800 m/kg / 4,375 yds/lb
7 wpc / 18 wpi

£4.25 - 25 gms
£12.75 - 100 gms

15 Camden Passage
London N1 8EA
020 7288 1160
Tube: Angel
www.loopknitting.com

# Loop

One of the most inspiring storefronts along the charming and historic Camden Passage—home to the world-famous Camden Passage antiques market—is Loop. Stepping into Loop is like stepping into someone's cosy home. Among the colourful yarn that fills wall-to-wall shelves is artwork by Parisiennes Sophie Digard and Nathalie Lété, as well as artful creatures by Julie Arkell, one of England's most celebrated folk artists. Mid-century furniture with barkcloth-covered cushions, draped with crocheted and knitted blankets simply add to the warmth. Vintage glass display cases and painted metal trolleys gracefully styled with all manner of knitting paraphernalia all give the inviting sense that you are not just at any shop, but at a place where you could comfortably sit chatting with a friend, knitting the hours away.

Perusing the vast range of books, patterns and haberdashery supplies is likely to keep any shopper busy browsing long before the yarn hits the needles. But customers who come strictly for the yarn are in luck. Owner Susan Cropper says, "coming into Loop is like being at the best indie yarn fair!" Not only is Loop the European Flagship shop for both Brooklyn Tweed and Quince and Co yarns and patterns, it has a tremendous range of hand-dyed yarns made in small batches from all over the world, including more than 100 colours of hand-dyed Madelinetosh yarn. Courses held at the shop range from beginner to master classes and have been taught by experienced knitters around the world, such as Stephen West, Melanie Berg and Hélène Magnússon.

# WINDSOR MITTS

BLUE SKY ALPACAS ROYAL PETITE KNITTING

SOCK YARN SWEATER
by Knitbot

Knit with one skein of Madeline
Tosh Sock in Candlewick
♡~♡
Sample Size = 0-6 months
❋~❋
3.5 mm needle

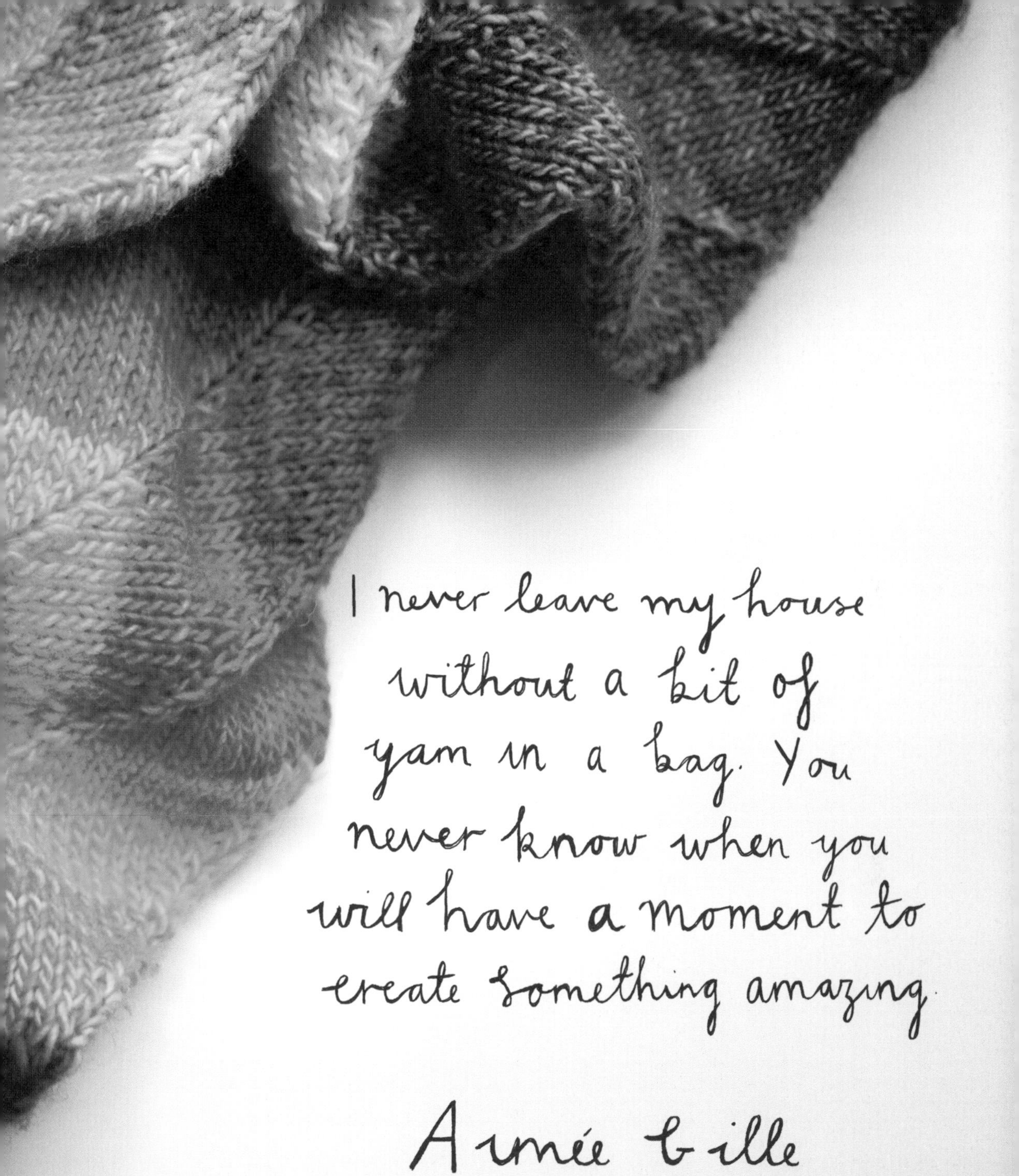

I never leave my house
without a bit of
yarn in a bag. You
never know when you
will have a moment to
create something amazing.

Aimée Gille

# SOUTH

Tourists often stick to Central London, rarely venturing south of the river—after all, what's down there anyway? A lot actually! Though the majority of London's fabric and knitting shops can be found north of the river, a few in South London are definitely worth the short trek, if not for the shops themselves then to experience how locals really live in this part of the city. What South London lacks in tourist attractions, it makes up for in its everyday character. Though many South London neighbourhoods are not on a tube line, they're often linked to the overground, which has equally easy access into the city. Many parts of South London have a cosy, laid back, village vibe. Some—like Brixton, with its African and Caribbean influences—are culturally diverse and a bit edgy, while others—like Herne Hill, which borders Brockwell Park—have a distinct family-friendly atmosphere. Forest Hill is a great neighbourhood for anyone who has a nostalgic beat in their heart: from the retro sweet shop, Sugar Mountain, to St David coffee house, where music plays on a record player, to time worn vintage shops such as The Montage and Dapper.

South London is also home to The Fashion and Textile Museum on Bermondsey Street, where fashion and fibre enthusiasts are likely to take a keen interest in the exhibits, workshops and courses, such as pattern cutting and tapestry weaving. In addition to the shops in this chapter that offer their own courses, other great places to get your stitch on in South London include author of *Love at First Stitch* Tilly Walnes' sewing school in West Dulwich, and The White Room sewing school in Brockley.

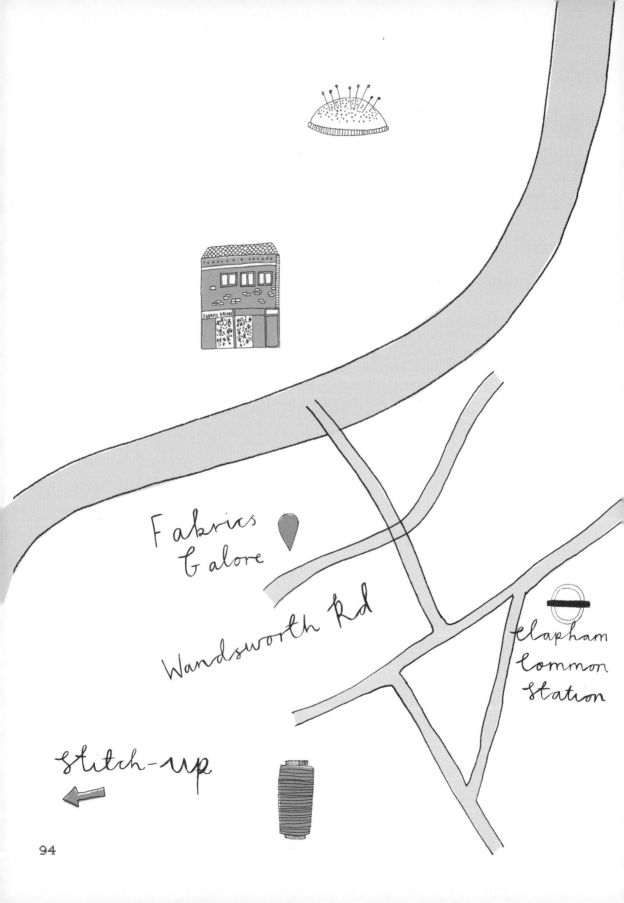

Fabrics
Galore

Wandsworth Rd

Clapham
Common
Station

stitch-up

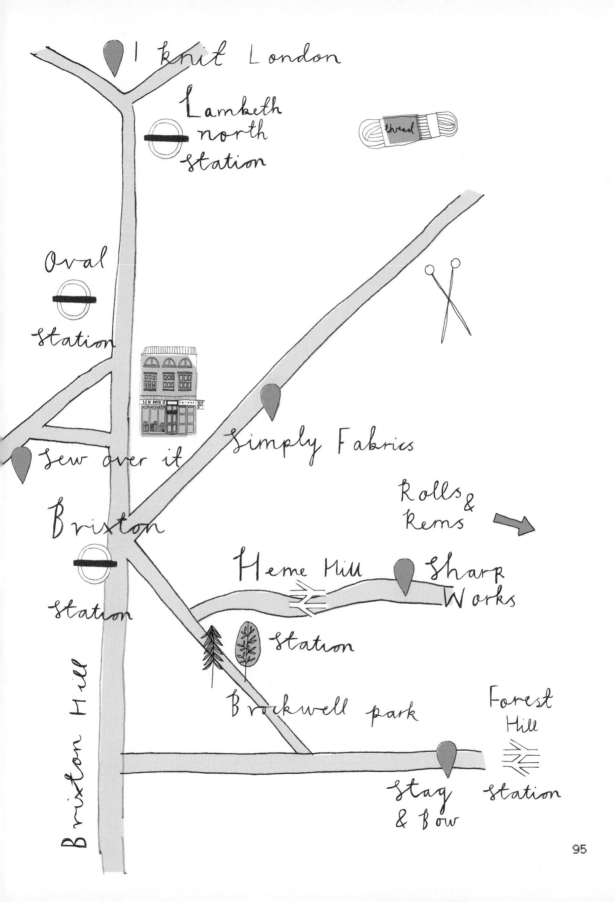

I Knit London

Lambeth north station

thread

Oval station

Sew over it

Simply Fabrics

Rolls & Rems

Brixton station

Heme Hill station

Sharp Works

Brixton Hill

Brockwell park

Forest Hill station

Stag & Bow

Debbie Bliss — Cashmerino Aran - £5.50
50g/90m/5mm Needles (55% Wool/33% Acrylic/12% Cashmere)

Rowan – A
100g\70m\10mm

Rowan – Lima - £7.50
50g\100m\5-5.5mm Needles (85% Baby Alpaca\8% Merino Wool\8% Nylon)

130 Arthur Road
London SW19 8AA
020 8944 6488
Tube: Wimbledon Park
www.stitchup.co.uk

# stitch-up

**XX** nstantly hooked on sewing at the age of seven, owner of Stitch-up,
**XX** Sandie Bonfield, turned a hobby into a life-long passion.
**XX** She spent many happy years working as a dressmaker before
taking a break to have a family. Disappointed at the loss of so many
traditional haberdashery shops, after her children grew a bit older,
Sandie felt it was time to encourage a resurgence of the high street
haberdashery, but with a modern approach.

Stitch-up is a patchwork crafter's dream. The shop is brimming
with 100 per cent cottons in floral, abstract and novelty prints,
the majority of which are sweet, colourful and fun. Sandie stocks
designer fabrics by Michael Miller, Riley Blake and Benartex, which
are not only used for quilting but for dressmaking, homewares
and craft projects too. They also have a dynamic range of yarns
including Lang yarns and Adriafil yarns made in Italy. Sandi
says another brand, Malabrigo, "is a perennial favourite with our
customers, with Lang Mille Colori coming a close second for gorgeous
multicoloured lace scarves".

Ribbons, trims, buttons, knitting needles and baskets filled with
pre-cut fat quarters cover a table in the centre of the cheerful
shop. Sandie aims to have haberdashery supplies to support any
project a crafter might have in mind. She also stocks these items to
support their range of courses which include courses for children
such as making pyjama shorts, making a piped cushion, and a hair
accessories course.

8 Dartmouth Road
London SE23 3XU
020 8291 4992
Overground: Forest Hill
www.stagandbow.com

# Stag & Bow

Just up from Forest Hill Overground station on Dartmouth Road is Stag & Bow, a haberdashery with a genuine sense of community. Lining the tall shelves of this cosy shop are vintage finds, such as pretty patterned teacups, vintage books and textiles, all mixed with handmade accessories from local designers, such as clutch purses made with 1960s fabrics, silkscreen printed cards and eclectic jewellery. Owners and partners, Cyrus and Pascale are quite the talented pair. Cyrus, with a background in woodworking and design, and Pascale, with a background in tailoring and weaving, are both passionate about the materials they use, how things are made and where they come from.

Downstairs at Stag & Bow is a fully functional textile studio, available for hire on an hourly or daily basis and offered for use as part of a membership at Stag & Bow. The studio has facilities for screen printing, weaving and a variety of dressmaking and tailoring needs. It also serves as a workshop space for a range of courses such as pattern making, feltmaking and tatting. Crafters are welcome to join in on craft night socials each month, where you can bring a project you are working on and enjoy the company of other crafters, all while sipping wine from a teacup.

The Craft
of the
Crochet
Hook

A BOOK OF NEW
IDEAS IN CROCHET
WORK OF VARIOU:
KINDS SHOWING NOVE:
METHODS OF APPLYING
THEM TO PERSONAL
AND HOUSEHOLD LINEN
AND HOME DECORATION

EDIT:
FLORA KLIC

30 cm
6.50 mm

30 cm
6 mm

KNITTI

ITCHLEY BROS

Simply Fabrics
57
020 3602 0723
www.simplyfabrics.net

NET/TULLE FROM
£1 PER METRE

PLASTIC CURTAIN
RINGS
5P TOP

LARGE IRON ON
BUTTERFLIES
£2.00 EACH

CLEAN BLIND
RINGS
5P EACH

SMALL IRON ON
BUTTERFLIES
80P EACH

NEEDLE
THREADERS
25P EACH

CHIFFON POLKA DOT
FLOWER
£1.00 EACH

GINGHAM & POLKA
DOT BOWS
10P EACH

LUREX ROSE
50P EACH

104

Simply Fabrics (Trimmings & Haberdashery)
48 Atlantic Road
London SW9 8JN
020 7733 2877
Tube: Brixton
www.simplyfabrics.london

Simply Fabrics (Suiting & Dress Fabrics)
57 Atlantic Road
London SW9 8PU
020 3602 0723
Tube: Brixton
www.simplyfabrics.london

# Simply Fabrics

**S**imply fabrics has two locations just down the street from each other—the haberdashery shop at 48 Atlantic Road and the fabric shop at 57 Atlantic Road. Owner Robert Chinman got his start selling fabrics in Walworth at the East Street Market. In 1988 he moved to Brixton and opened the location at 48 Atlantic Road, expanding with the fabric shop in 2012. The haberdashery is great for the nuts and bolts of a project, zippers in particular. "Zips, zips and more zips. We sell a huge range of zips", says Robert. Not only does the Simply Fabrics haberdashery offer a huge range of zips in a rainbow of colours, but they also sell a variety of other supplies that sewists and crafters will find useful such as interfacing, cotton wadding and twill tape.

The fabric shop can be excellent if you are happy to dig to find some treasures, or if you are just in the market for a deal. Customers who come in on a Friday are likely to have first dibs on the new stock that arrives weekly—which could include gems by designers such as Paul Smith—but you can always find competitive prices on linen, pure wool, shirting, jersey, printed and solid cottons. If you work up an appetite loading your boot with bargains, you are in luck because some of the best food in the city is at Brixton Village Market, an uber hip, covered food market packed with excellent tiny restaurants, just a few steps from Simply Fabrics.

SHARP WORKS

Iton Road  Haberdashery  Knitting Yarns  0207 58

220 Railton Road
London SE24 0JT
020 7738 7668
National Rail: Herne Hill
www.sharpworks.co.uk

# Sharp Works

Tucked on the curvy, village-like Railton Road in Herne Hill is Sharp Works. You can't miss the cheerful pom poms and bunting that are on colourful rotation in the window throughout the year. Thoughtfully styled with a few vintage display pieces and vintage cinema seats, this neighbourhood knitting shop, owned by Susan Sharp, stocks a reliable selection of yarn by Debbie Bliss, Rowan, Artesano and Louisa Harding. They also have a useful selection of haberdashery supplies, which includes tools from companies such as Knit Pro, Brittany and Clover, and a variety of patterns, including their own original designs. Customers can also browse a great selection of books both for the beginner just getting a start on the needles and for someone ready to take on the challenge of Fair Isle. Susan is happy to talk to anyone perplexed by a knitting problem or to simply help customers choose suitable materials for a particular pattern.

Courses ranging from knitting in the round using circular knitting needles to cabling are part of a handful of evening classes offered at Sharp Works. Beginner and granny square crochet courses are also part of their rotating course schedule. If the weather is nice, make your visit to Sharp Works all the more enjoyable by indulging in some artisan picnic fare at Dugard and Daughters Larder and stroll over to Brockwell Park to enjoy a bit of knitting while you nosh.

52–54 Lavender Hill
London SW11 5RH
020 7738 9589
National Rail: Clapham Junction
www.fabricsgalore.co.uk

# Fabrics Galore

Not even 30 minutes after opening on any day of the week, Fabrics Galore is buzzing with customers, many with pattern in hand, dashing from one fabric to the next, admiring them while trying to choose the perfect fit for their project. Clapham locals are especially lucky to have this fantastic fabric store in their area, but ask any regular customer and you will learn that people don't mind travelling from afar to shop at Fabrics Galore. One step inside and it is easy to see why. With a collection that's guided by an eye for print, colour and natural fibres, Fabrics Galore offers a high quality selection at very reasonable prices.

Owner Paul Johnston says "you can never have enough of the basics: good quality cottons, great soft furnishing linens, taffeta, georgettes, fleece and felt", all of which they sell on a daily basis. Customers flock to Fabrics Galore for many of those fabric staples, but a few highlights of the shop are its extensive range of past-season Liberty Tana Lawns, which are available at irresistible prices, and Alexander Henry fabrics, which all start with a hand painted design. Paul's strong relationship with suppliers allows him to purchase fabrics at great wholesale prices, a benefit which is then passed on to his customers.

Though the majority of their merchandise is fabric, they also sell a great range of patterns and have a small haberdashery section. If a visit to the shop is beyond your reach, they sell many of their fabrics online and at numerous quilt and craft markets throughout the UK. Their website is updated regularly with market dates.

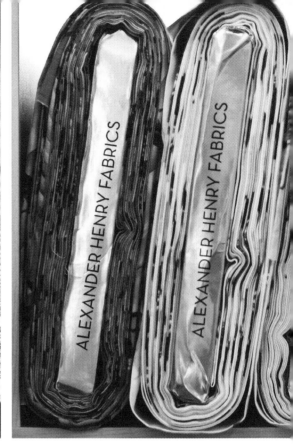

ALEXANDER HENRY FABRICS

ALEXANDER HENRY FABRICS

ALEXANDER HENRY FABRICS

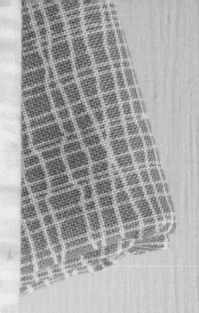

111 Lewisham High Street
London SE13 6AT
020 8852 8686
National Rail and DLR: Lewisham
www.rollsandrems.com

# Rolls & Rems

Rolls & Rems have three locations: one in Edmonton, one in Holloway, and one South London's Lewisham. All three carry similar stock, but the Lewisham location is the largest of the three. At the entrance of their stores is a large box of remnants which reflects Rolls and Rems' great reputation for excellent remnant cuts—often end of roll cuts in multiple metre lengths offered at incredible prices (many of the multiple metre pieces are marked at the price of just one metre). With those bargains to be had, it's easy to leave the shop with heaps of fabric just from the scraps, but with very reasonable prices on their regular stock too, customers rarely stop at the remnant bin.

The Rolls & Rems shops have a similar organisation to each other, with fabrics grouped in sections of like materials. The Holloway location, for example, has one wall of shelves that displays satin, lace, voile, chiffon and silk fabrics; and an opposite wall displays cottons in solid, check, dot, stripe, floral and abstract designs—great for both for patchwork and dressmaking.

While their cotton prints may not come from leading modern designers, they do offer a great variety of designs. Upstairs are jersey fabrics in solids, stripes and dots as well as ticking, metallic and technical fabrics, and curtain and upholstery fabrics. They also carry a great range or ribbon, trim, buttons and zips. So, though Rolls & Rems may not be a destination fabric shop, for dressmakers and crafters interested in fabrics at great prices, it's worth a trip.

OUR CLASSES

BEGINNERS
· Intro to sewing
· Button me cushion

DRESSMAKING
· Intro to dressmaking
· Intro to commercial patterns
· Ultimate shift dress

ACCESSORIES
· Leather handbag
· Weekend holder

NEEDLECRAFT
· Intro to knitting
· Beginner's crochet

PATTERN CUTTING
· Draft basic blocks

78 Landor Road
London SW9 9PH
020 7326 0376
Tube: Clapham North
Overground: Clapham High Street
www.sewoverit.co.uk

# Sew over it

On a gloomy winter day, a trip into Sew Over It's Clapham branch will make any crafter feel like a kid in a candy store. Against white walls are bold blue letters saying "just keep sewing, sewing, sewing" and "sewing soothes the soul... or something like that". Shelves are lined with bright, cheerful fabrics in florals checks and dots, as well as an equally colourful selection of wool, complemented by a small but beautiful choice of haberdashery supplies, filled with helpful tools to get you stitching in one of their many classes. They also sell a diverse range of their own popular dressmaking patterns.

Owner Lisa Comfort opened the sewing cafe in 2011 with a goal to get people back in touch with their sewing side, and the Sew Over It sewing machines have been humming ever since. After studying at the London College of Fashion, Lisa worked for British designer Bruce Oldfield and then bridal couture designer Phillipa Lepley. She's now sharing her years of experience with students eager to learn or improve their sewing skills. Classes at Sew Over It range from an introduction to sewing, to advanced dressmaking. They also offer courses for the home, such as sewing curtains and roman blinds, and a few helpful mini classes to tackle topics such as the ever intimidating zip. Though Sew Over It is primarily a sewing lounge, knitters are also welcome and will find their knitting club quite handy for improving skills in sock making, intarsia knitting and cabling.

Lisa is the author of a wonderful book for beginner sewists, *Sew It, Wear It, Love It*, which is filled with easy-to-follow instructions for updating your wardrobe with simple customisation techniques and making your own original accessories. North Londoners will be pleased to know that there is a second Sew Over It location in Islington.

116

SEWING SOOTHES THE SOUL... OR SOMETHING LIKE THAT

SINGER

SEW OVER IT

1940's Tea Dress

117

SOCKS à la carte Colorwork

SOLEFULL SOCKS
Knitting from the Ground Up
Betty Salpekar

IN SHEEP'S CLOTHING

sock innovation

beads & buttons

anna zilborg

I Knit
or Dye
www.iknit.org.uk

106 Lower Marsh
London SE1 7AB
020 7261 1338
Tube or National Rail: Waterloo
www.iknit.org.uk

# I knit London

Lower Marsh, home to Lower Marsh Saturday Market, is a pedestrian friendly street lined with excellent independent shops, cafes and pubs. Just a short stroll from Waterloo Station, this street is often buzzing with shoppers, especially at lunchtime. Among cafes, boutiques, and vintage shops is I Knit London. Nearly impossibly to miss thanks to its bold yellow and black sign, this knitting shop is a long standing hub for local knitting groups.

Director and manager Gerard Allt says that I Knit London started with a small knitting group in Vauxhall who were "soon moving from pub to pub meeting new people and making friends". A passion for wool and meeting other like-minded knitters motivated Gerard to open a stall at Spitalfields Market selling a variety of needles and a few interesting yarns. After a little more than a year selling at the market, he opened a shop in Vauxhall. I Knit London outgrew its first shop location in Vauxhall after just two years and moved to its current space on Lower Marsh in 2008.

The extensive selection of yarn is a big draw for customers, including their own exclusive line—I Knit or Dye—a hand painted luxury yarn. Knitters go to I Knit London not just to shop but also "for the atmosphere of the knitting group", says Gerard. "I Knit has always believed community is really important", he says. He brings people together weekly with three groups each week: a knitting group, a book club and a cake club. I Knit London is also fully licensed to serve adult beverages, so instead of the knitters heading to a pub these days, Gerard has brought the pub to the knitters, with wine and cider the most popular tipples.

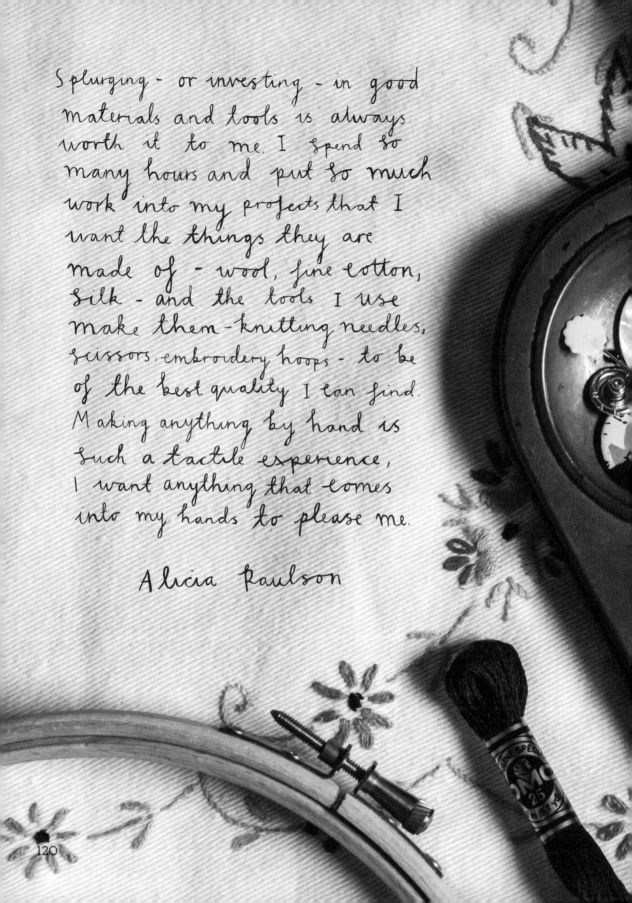

Splurging - or investing - in good materials and tools is always worth it to me. I spend so many hours and put so much work into my projects that I want the things they are made of - wool, fine cotton, silk - and the tools I use make them - knitting needles, scissors, embroidery hoops - to be of the best quality I can find. Making anything by hand is such a tactile experience, I want anything that comes into my hands to please me.

Alicia Paulson

THE SNOWDROP
TWO HOLE COVERED BACK BUTTON

TRADE MARK
CROSS SCISSORS

A STRONG RELIABLE BUTTON

SILVER PLATED BRASS FRAMES

MADE IN ENGLAND

# EAST

An area rich in diversity, East London is edgy, arty, a bit earthy and uber hip—a hot spot for twenty-something creatives. It is also an area that celebrates contrasts; where many shops on the popular Brick Lane are rough and worn like This Shop Rocks (a vintage shop cluttered with second-hand gems), a number of shops on nearby Redchurch Street take the opposite approach. Take for instance housewares shop Labour and Wait, which emphasises simplicity in its contemporary, functional design.

East London is an excellent area for fabric and knitting supplies, not only for places included in this chapter, but for a number of other gems that sparkle in East London's neighbourhoods. Just outside Dalston Mill Fabrics are a handful of great material and haberdashery stalls on Ridley Road like the 50p fabric stall and a few others that sell some beautifully bold, graphic African prints; and U and I Trimmings in Dalston is perfect for sewing supply basics. HC Bhopal on Brick Lane is a fabric shop packed so full there is hardly room to walk the length of the store, and while it may not be one worth making a special trip for, it's certainly worth a peek if you are in the area. On Quaker Street, just around the corner from Brick Lane, the discount fabric warehouse Crescent Trading has loads of bargain pieces and is particularly great for suiting wools. Knitters will enjoy the Good Yarn Stall at the Sunday Spitalfields Market, a stall with a focus on yarns from hand-dyed to cashmere.

Further east, Walthamstow is a fabric haven similar to that of Goldhawk Road in the west. Walthamstow may be at the end of the Victoria Line, but hardcore fabric lovers—especially those in the market for bargains—will be giddy over heaps of stash- and confidence-building fabrics to be found at places like Saeed Fabrics and a number of stalls at the Walthamstow Market.

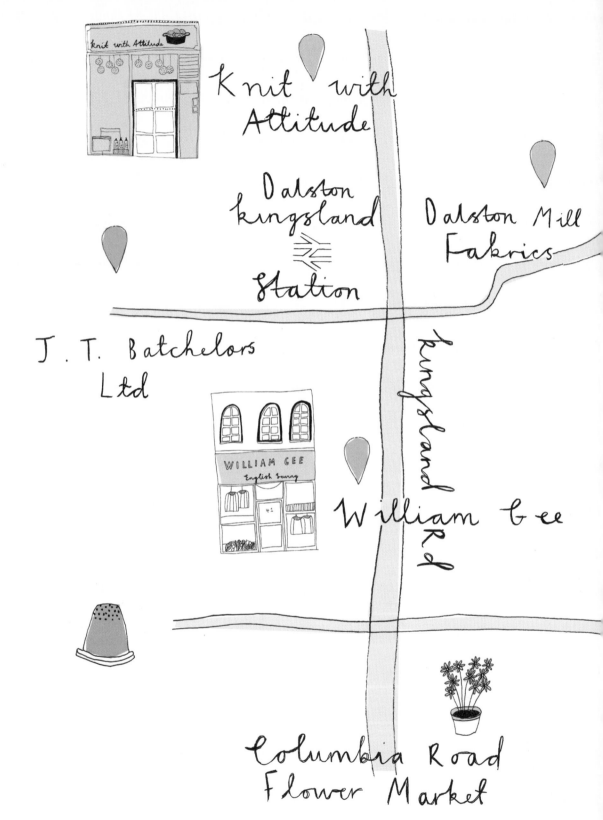

Knit with Attitude

Dalston kingsland Station

Dalston Mill Fabrics

J. T. Batchelors Ltd

WILLIAM GEE
English Sewing
41

Kingsland Rd

William Gee

Columbia Road Flower Market

Lower Clapton Road

Wild and woolly

London fields

Station

Fabrications

Victoria park

Bethnal green

Station

Prick your finger

116 Lower Clapton Road
London E5 0QX
020 8985 5231
Overground: Hackney Downs, Clapton
www.wildandwoollyshop.co.uk

# Wild and Woolly

Anna Feldman has dabbled in various other fibre arts over the years, but it is her interest in knitting that has endured since childhood. She became more enthusiastic about her knitting hobby as she lost interest in looking at a computer screen all day. "I began to add detail to a fantasy I had about opening a local wool shop where knitters would be welcomed regardless of skill, and helped on their way with whatever support and supplies they needed", she says. Today that fantasy is a reality in her welcoming knitting shop in Hackney.

At the entrance of the shop is a lovely table where knitters are invited to sit and have a cup of tea while working on their knitting. Anna is happy to help anyone struggling with a project. "I find that a cup of tea and a methodical look through it all usually puts things right", she explains. Anna prides herself on carrying needles of every size and being the sole London stockist of a handful of fantastic yarns such as Baa Ram Ewe's Titus, Kettle Yarn Company's Islington, Wimbledon and Beyul, and Kalinka's 100 per cent linen.

Customers who might be a bit bored with their yarn stash at home are welcome to use the Wild and Woolly "stash depot" to sell their unwanted yarn in exchange for store credit. Anna also offers a 10 per cent discount the second Wednesday of every month during her "late-night knitty lock-ins" where locals enjoy the company of other knitters while enjoying tea and cake to their heart's content.

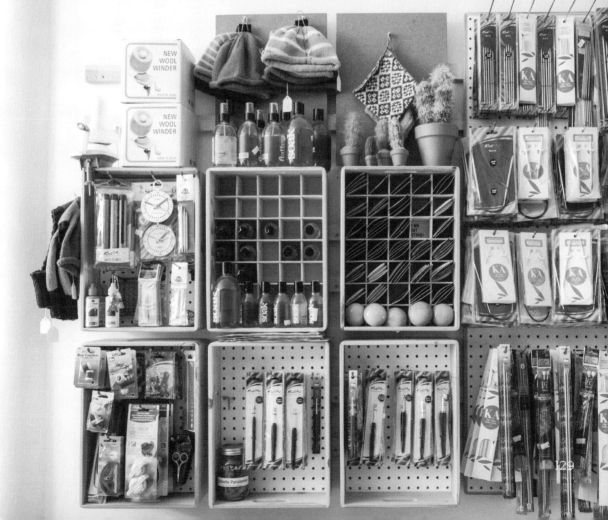

# J.T. Batchelors Ltd

✗✗n an unassuming location along a brick-lined mews is J.T. Batchelors, a leather supplier that sells a range of leathers and leather working tools. J.T. Batchelors' cave-like space, behind green warehouse doors, is plain and simple in its presentation of the materials it houses. Metal and plastic shelving units throughout the warehouse are stacked with leathers of cow-, sheep-, pig- and goatskins in variety of colours and thicknesses. From simple brown or black leathers to metallic silver or neon green, if it is leather you are looking for, you won't have trouble finding it at J.T. Batchelors. Their thinnest leather at 0.5mm is a sheepskin skiver leather, perfect for projects such as book binding; the thickest at 4mm is a cow shoulder leather, perfect for belts and harnesses. They specialise in vegetable-tanned skins and all of their skins are meat by-products, so none of their leathers are from animals slaughtered solely for their skins. Customers will also find an excellent selection of tools and accessories including needles and thread suitable for various leathers as well as punch pliers, clicker knives, D-rings and numerous styles and size buckles.

Next door to J.T. Batchelors is The Little Workshop, a separate business but one that works closely with J.T. Batchelors to provide a workspace for individuals and small businesses. The workshop offers space to cut, sew and finish leather projects that range from simple belts to smart satchels, and is available for hire on an hourly basis.

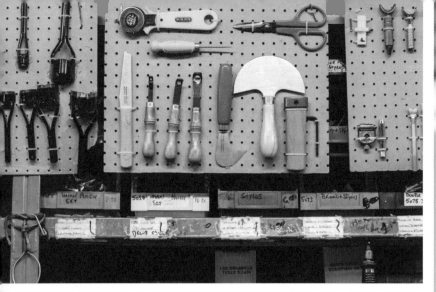
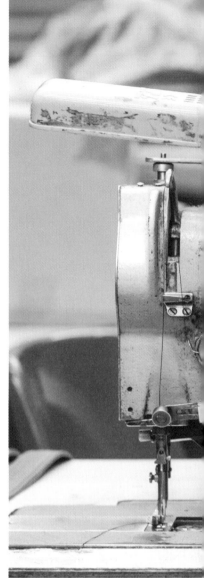

END     50g Merino Wool/Silk     DK     £9.00

O     50g Merino/Alpaca     DK     £5.00

STITCH & STORY
25CM / 12MM
100% bamboo

7.0mm

127 Stoke Newington High Street
London N16 0PH
020 7998 3282
National Rail: Stoke Newington
www.knitwithattitude.com

# Knit with Attitude

Conscious crafting—with a focus on environmentally friendly and ethically produced products—is the prevailing philosophy at Knit with Attitude. This bright, modern shop is shared with Of Cabbages and Kings, an art and design shop that sells merchandise by independent UK artists and designers. The two enterprises complement each other, fitting together seamlessly in both their aesthetic and ethos.

In the early 2000s, when blogs were taking off, owner of Knit with Attitude, May Linn "Maya" Bang says she was "fascinated with how young people embraced the old technique, making it their own through new expressions like 'political yarn bombing' and 'knitting activism'". She says this exciting knitting revolution coincided with an increased concern for the environment and a desire to use more sustainable products. She was thrilled to be a part of the exciting changes in the world of knitting.

The name itself—Knit with Attitude—stems from this passion to keep her products ethical and environmentally respectful. Maya says she spends a significant amount of time researching the products she sells to make certain they are responsible products made by companies conscious about their own manufacturing process. She carries yarn by The Fibre Company, Susan Crawford Vintage and Viking of Norway, to name a few, along with haberdashery, books, patterns, gifts and accessories.

While the philosophy of Knit with Attitude may be popular with a younger generation, Maya aims to bridge the gap between generations of knitters. She has found it is important to carry on-trend yarns and patterns for younger generations but at the same time "to honour the experience and detailed knowledge of those who have been knitting 'forever'".

135

CRAZY SEXY WOOL
100% PERUVIAN WOOL
MADE IN PERU
WWW.WOOLANDTHEGANG.COM

# WOOL AND THE GANG

#MADEUNIQUE

200 GR
80M / 87YDS
3 STITCHES PER 1"/ 2.5 CM
NEEDLE SIZE 15 MM

SPECIAL OFFER £3 p/m

69–73 Ridley Road
London E8 3NP
020 7249 4129
Overground: Dalston Kingsland
or Dalston Junction
www.dalstonmillfabrics.co.uk

# Dalston Mill Fabrics

A visit to Dalston Mill Fabrics requires a bit of confidence and patience: confidence to ask for what you want and patience to receive it. Although the staff are very friendly and helpful, their merchandise is stacked almost as high as Jack's beanstalk. Most of the fabric isn't marked with a price, or if it is, it is often too high up to reach to see the price, so it is best to arrive knowing what you are looking for, and how much you expect to pay. Though you might need to wait a few minutes while someone climbs a ladder to reach the fabric you want, fabrics that are out of reach are available to see and feel on sample strips that dangle from hooks near their corresponding bolt.

Dalston Mill Fabrics have an enormous and diverse range of fabrics—many at reasonable prices—the majority of which are in the main room at the entrance. Lace, wool, cotton, satin, brocade, cashmere and leather are packed in this cavernous space from floor to ceiling. Several smaller rooms which branch off in the back and to the side are equally jammed with fabrics; one entire room is devoted to wools and suiting fabric; another is filled with organza, georgette, crepe de chine, satin and silk fabrics; and yet another at the back is strictly for the Mill's extensive range of haberdashery supplies, where customers will find buttons, trims, zippers, sequins, elastics, dyes, feathers and a small selection of yarn.

The Dalston Mill Fabrics website features many of their fabrics and is updated regularly with the most recent arrivals. Samples can be purchased for 50p, and all customers receive a ten per cent discount online.

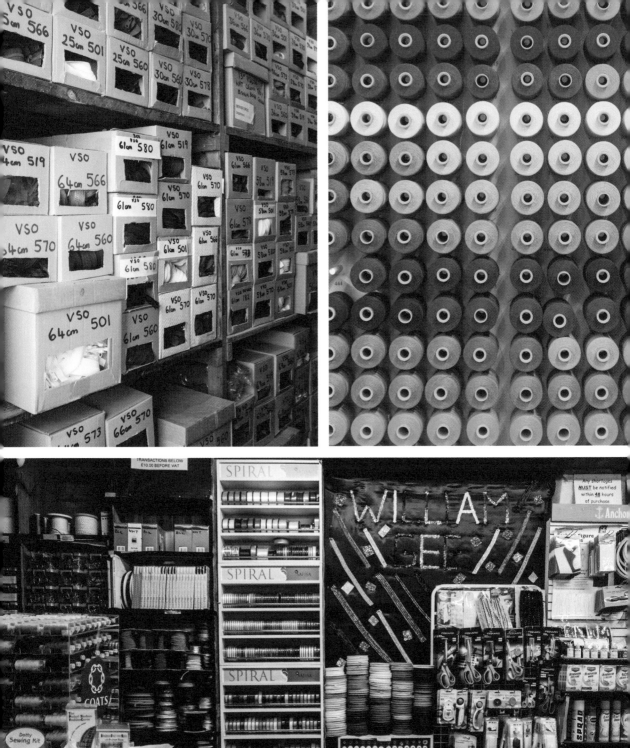

520–522 Kingsland Road
London E8 4AR
020 7254 2451
Overground: Dalston Junction
www.williamgee.co.uk

# William Gee

Opened in 1906, William Gee, a family-run business now in its fourth generation, is one of a handful of haberdashery shops that remain in an area of Hackney that was historically a centre for the rag trade. Most evidence of that former industry is long gone, but stepping into William Gee is like stepping back in time. Just inside the doors is a wood-panelled room with service counters on both sides. Contrary to our modern shopping habits, this is not the kind of place where one can browse products, picking up items along the way, instead, at William Gee customers go to the counter and ask a salesperson for what they need. The salesperson then retrieves the merchandise for the customers—continuing the traditional service the store has operated since its inception.

The products displayed behind the counter give little indication of the vast number actually available at the shop, but the salespeople know their stock by heart and just beyond the walls of the sales floor are numerous rooms connected like a maze through narrow hallways and filled floor to ceiling with items. William Gee's longstanding and thriving wholesale business accounts for the majority of their large quantities of merchandise, but they are happy to provide retail customers with smaller orders as well. Pattern paper, bias binding, interfacing, sewing thread, elastics, fasteners, and a huge variety of YKK zips are some of the most commonly requested items, though they also offer speciality items such as tailor's canvas and Shoben block patterns.

Their regularly updated website—the modern style of which is in sharp contrast to the traditional approach of their brick and mortar shop—features helpful photos and informative descriptions of many of the products they sell in-store, all of which can be delivered to your door within three days in the UK.

141

260 Globe Road
London E2 0JD
020 8981 2560
Tube: Bethnal Green
www.prickyourfinger.com

# Prick your Finger

**W**ithout even stepping into Prick Your Finger, the shop's name might give you a clue that this is no stiff knitting shop, but one with a great sense of humour. Owner Rachel Mathews has created a laid-back atmosphere where local Hackney knitters feel right at home. The floor-to-ceiling wood interior has a warm and worn vibe that will make you feel like you have stepped into a cool little knitting cabin in the woods. The earthy tone of the rustic decor is also reflected in the unique collection of recycled yarns for sale, such as carpet yarn and silk sari yarn. Rachel's light-hearted take on her craft is revealed in a crocheted glitter ball hanging from the ceiling in the main room and in a crocheted toilet filled with bargain bin yarn. Passionate about British yarn manufacturing, Prick Your Finger stocks British yarns exclusively. One popular line is Devon-based Knit By Numbers in over 80 colours, as well as Shetland Spindrift in 50 colours. They also dye and spin their own line of yarns, one of which is a rainbow cotton yarn, having a look similar to that of a rag rug—a bit tattered, confetti-coloured and soft.

Prick Your Finger has a brilliant selection of vintage patterns and a number of indie knitting books, including Rachel's own books *Knitorama: 25 Great and Glam Things to Knit* and *Hookorama: 25 Fabulous Things to Crochet*. She also sells locally handmade jewellery and art from designers such as Max Alexander who makes quirky craft-themed jewellery, and Fleur Oakes who creates delightful miniature haberdashery kits in Victorian-style domes. Courses range from beginner knitting and crochet to more specific introductions to spinning and macrame.

144

CARPET YARN
£7 per 100g
100% Tough Wool!

Hand dyed
"Terribly Tastefull"
BFL ARAN-
£10/100g

Rachael Matthews
**Knitorama**
25 Great &
Glam Things
to Knit

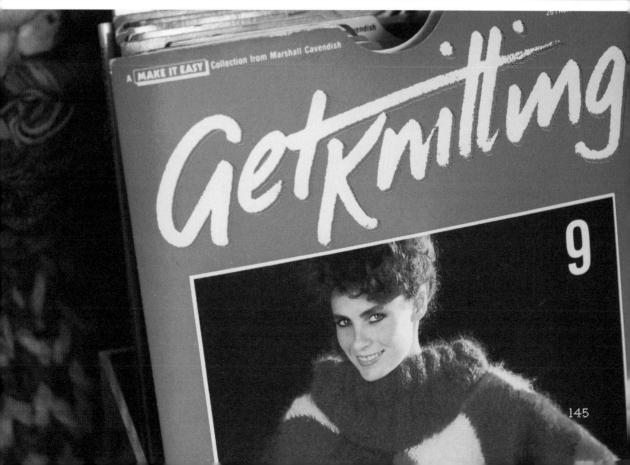

A MAKE IT EASY Collection from Marshall Cavendish

GetKnitting

9

145

35

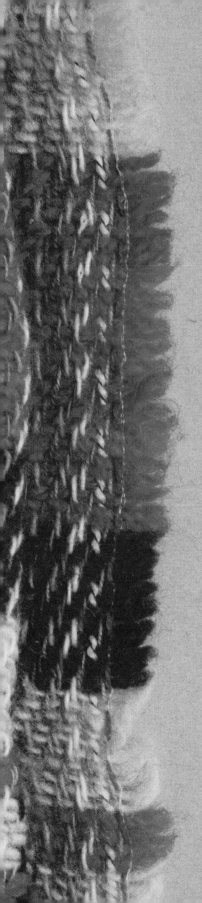

7 Broadway Market
London E8 4PH
020 7275 8043
Overground: London Fields, Hoxton
Tube: Bethnal Green
www.fabrications1.co.uk

# Fabrications

**XXX** f any one knitting shop in London embodies the expression "waste not, want not" it's Barley Massey's shop Fabrications on Broadway Market. After studying textile design at Goldsmiths College, working on textiles for film and television and longing for her own textile studio, Barley grasped an opportunity in the 1990s to open a shop on the then rather run down market street. Taking up one of the empty storefronts while the local council strived to enliven and re-energise the area, Barley had a chance to "not only have a studio, but a window unto the world". Her ambitious move paid off; today Fabrications continues to contribute to what is now a thriving, culturally buzzing part of East London.

Fabrications has always had the aim "to inspire, enhance and demonstrate art and design's potential for social and environmental change", and sells an excellent selection of British, eco-friendly, upcycled and unusual yarns by companies such as West Yorkshire Spinners, Erika Knight and Mirasol. In addition to their own recycled multi-plied chunky yarns, and wool spun by local spinners, they are also the sole stockist of Wool-n-Dance macro knitting needles.

But Fabrications isn't simply a knitting shop. Barley says she likes to think of it instead as a "mini department store". Customers can purchase one of Barley's many original upcycled homewares and accessories, such as a tube cushion made from hand-woven upcycled bicycle inner tubes, or craft kits from her "rethink rubbish" series, which, she explains, are like "a mini-workshop in a bag". She's also proud of her "remember me" service where she offers a service to upcycle sentimental garments into a quilt, throw or a cushion.

A STITCH IN TIME SAVES NINE

148

€12.50

rethink rubbish
a creative and inspirational kit by Barley Massey

barley massey

sustainable
gift wrapping

ON..... Thursday

THIS SAT   A. Learn to Knit an
           M. 'Entrelac' Scarf
           P. Beginners Knitting (part 1)
           M.

THIS SUN   A. Introduction to garment
           M. Alterations
           P. 'Refresh your Wardrobe'
           M.

Coming up ......
· 'provisional Driving'- intro to using a sewing ma
· 'Improvers sewing' (zips, buttonholes, bindings)
· Design + make your own 2 colourway Mittens

149

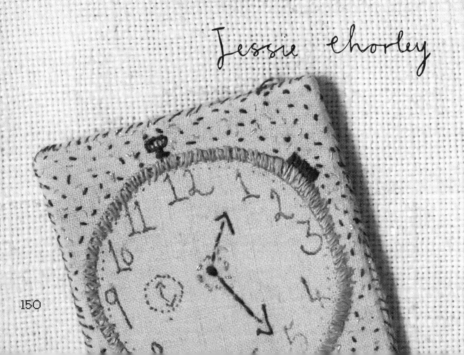

As a collector and maker I am drawn to fabrics that already hold, and are deeply embedded with an existing narrative. I particularly like working with details from clothing - collars, cuffs, and the insides of old worn jacket pockets are my perfect starting point and inspiration.

Jessie Chorley

With areas as diverse as Kensington—think tree-lined streets and smart independent boutiques—and the urban shopping area of Shepherd's Bush, which includes the colossal Westfield Mall, West London defies any one description. In the northwest of the area is Little Venice, a slice of picturesque waterways where Regent's Canal and the Grand Union Canal meet. Slightly south of that is Portobello Road, which delights tourists with its antique shops and weekend market. And the area has plenty of open space too, with beautiful green spaces including Richmond Park and Kew Gardens.

While West London offers many interesting choices for a day out, it's Goldhawk Road where fabric lovers can easily spend an entire day. With more than a dozen fabric shops concentrated on one street within a half a mile from each other, Goldhawk Road is a hotspot for local fabric enthusiasts. In contrast to the pricier fabric shops of Central London, these shops often have bargain prices while still supplying quality products. The sheer variety of materials for sale on Goldhawk Road will keep fabric-lovers happy. Unfortunately many shops on Goldhawk Road are in jeopardy of losing their spaces to developers who have plans to transform the area, but most of the businesses have plans to relocate nearby, so keep an eye out for the any changes taking place.

Any textile enthusiast with West London at their disposal should take a peek inside the V&A Museum. Among its impressive exhibits of art and design, this beautiful institution holds the national textiles and fashion collection—an archive of fabrics, knitting, embroidery and tapestry pieces dating as far back as 3,000 years. Also in this region of the city are a few great shops for anyone on a mission to find beads: Lyndon's Stitch and Beads on Portobello Road and Creative Beadcraft on Brewer Street.

classic
Testiles

A one
Fabrics

Shepherd's
Bush
Station

Goldhawk Road

A to Z
Fabrics

Goldhawk
Road
Station

Holland Road

Shaukat
& co

Old Brompton Rd

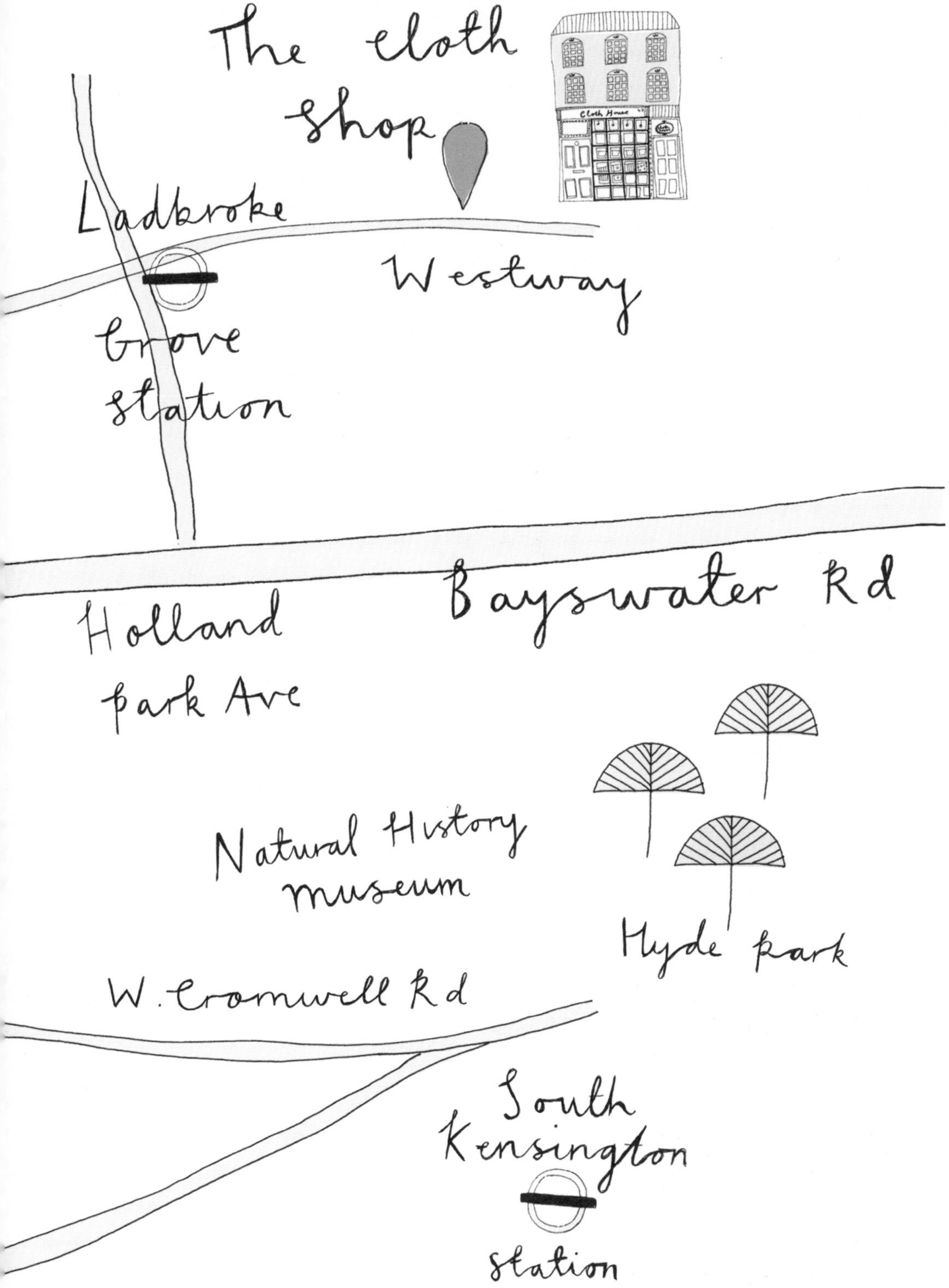

The cloth shop

Ladbroke

Westway

Grove
Station

Bayswater Rd

Holland
Park Ave

Natural History
Museum

Hyde Park

W. Cromwell Rd

South
Kensington

Station

# shaukat & co

For Liberty fabric admirers, there may be no better place in London to shop than Shaukat & Co on Old Brompton Road. Sewists enamoured with Liberty prints find Shaukat & Co to be a tremendous resource for a diverse range of Liberty fabrics at a price that won't do quite as much damage to your wallet as shopping at Liberty itself. Upon first entering you might wonder what all the fuss is about; while the two main ground floor rooms house numerous fabrics including wools, solid cottons, silks, dressmaking and crafting cottons, it is downstairs that you will find a world of Liberty.

Downstairs feels like a bunker of connected rooms, only instead of a lifetime's supply of food, you will feast your eyes on a lifetime's supply of Liberty fabrics. Rooms are filled with not only the entire range of Liberty classic cotton Tana Lawns, including current and a few past-season variations, but also Liberty print jersey, corduroy, twill, silk, crepe de chine and oilcloth—all of which are discounted by nearly 20 per cent.

Shaukat & Co are almost as well known for their hands-off approach to service as they are for their Liberty fabrics; you could easily be there 30 minutes without any acknowledgement. While the service may not seem initially warm and welcoming, if you do have questions or need help, there are numerous salespeople available to assist customers and answer any questions. They also have a significant number of fabrics available online.

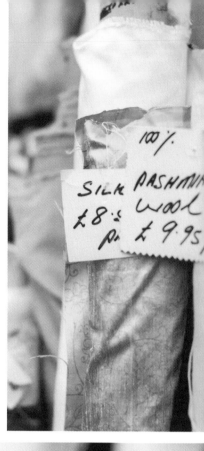

100%.
SILK PASHMINA
£8.95 WOOL
Pa £9.95

# classic Textiles

If you are interested in picking up some great silk fabric at reasonable prices, Classic Textiles is one of the best places for silks on Goldhawk Road. While their out-dated website may look a bit drab, the fabrics you will find at Classic Textiles are far from it. The shop consists of two floors, both of which are long and narrow, so narrow in fact that there's hardly room to turn around. Unlike most fabric stores that have large tables for cutting fabric, the salespeople in this slim shop cut standing at the roll. Rolls of fabric seem to jut out in every direction and with a staff of at least six at any given time, shopping in Classic Textiles is a tight squeeze, but one that's worth it.

In addition to a huge variety of silks, at Classic Textiles customers will find Liberty cotton prints, linen, denim, crepe and lace, and wool all at reasonable prices. This shop, like the majority of shops on Goldhawk Road is great for many of the staples for dressmaking, tailoring and costume design. Owner Aniza Meghani says the shop caters for anyone from home dressmakers looking for fabrics at great prices to film industry designers looking for interesting, quality materials. Every now and again customers will find real gems from big name designers. Aniza is pleased that they are often able to offer past-season and surplus designer fabrics from designers such as Missoni and Prada. In the 34 years Aniza's family has owned the shop, she says "we've never had the need to advertise; our name sells itself by word of mouth".

50–52 Goldhawk Road
London W12 8DH
020 8740 7349
Tube: Goldhawk Road

# A one Fabrics

As with most fabric shops on Goldhawk Road, A One Fabrics looks a little worse for wear on the outside. Inside the shop, though, one will find a generous space neatly stocked with a huge range of great fabrics. A One Fabrics is one of the must-visit shops on Goldhawk Road for fashion students, crafters, dressmakers and tailors. While there is a lot of overlap in the stock of the shops in the area, this one is reliable for a great selection of jersey, wool and cotton fabrics. The shop is divided by a wall creating two main rooms. One houses silk, linen, lace, brocade, embroidered, beaded and technical fabrics. The room opposite is filled with cotton, jersey, wool and felt. Within each category is great variety—cottons, for example, are available in solids, checks, dots, stripes, florals and abstract prints; jerseys in like manner come in a range of colours and prints; linens in a multitude of colours and weights. Both rooms are neat and tidy with plenty of room to browse the fabrics.

The staff are helpful and quite knowledgeable of their stock and sometimes willing to offer a discount beyond the prices listed, so be sure to ask the best price on your fabric. Also, if you find an imperfection on your fabric of choice, be sure to point it out and you will likely be offered a discount on the purchase as well.

Super Bargain
Crepes
150cm
wide £3.99 mtr
only

# A to Z Fabrics

Above the entryway to A to Z Fabrics is the word "sale", and indeed one can find many fabrics at great prices here. "Special offer" and "bargain" can be found on tags and signs dotted throughout the shop—but these signs are permanent, indicating consistently reasonable prices. The shop is a bit smaller than a few other fabric shops on Goldhawk Road, but it does offer a great selection of fabrics, with a terrific selection of silks in particular.

The shop is neatly arranged on three levels. At ground level are the majority of the fabrics: crepe, chiffon, silk, satin, velvet and cotton fabrics, arranged by style and colour. A few steps above this floor is a second level with wool, lace, beaded, and a few technical fabrics. The smaller lower ground floor is filled primarily with varied types of denim and linen fabrics. At A to Z Fabrics there's also has a small selection of Liberty prints and a number of great shirting fabrics too. The staff are friendly and happy to assist customers with any queries.

# The cloth shop

**P**ortobello Road is well-known for its antiques market, where tourists flock to admire collections of silver, china, enamelware, vintage cameras and clothes, and all manner of second-hand bric-a-brac. While prices aimed at tourists are often prohibitive, that doesn't stop throngs of people pouring into Notting Hill every Saturday. Over the years more and more chain stores have moved onto Portobello Road wanting to cash in on the guaranteed foot traffic. Where the street was once packed with independent shops, those appear to be fewer and fewer each year. Though many tourists will wear out before reaching the north end of Portobello Road, it's this section that retains Portobello's old character and charm, with more independent shops and restaurants than chain storès, and with antique and vintage stalls that are a bit edgier than the more polished stalls at the southern end.

The Cloth Shop is at the top of this more northern part of the road and a great place to start a stroll down Portobello Road. Sam and Susie Harley first opened The Cloth Shop in Soho in 1983 and moved to their current location in 1992. Having started with a focus on tailoring and dressmaking fabrics, today The Cloth Shop has many fabrics that are ideal for homewares and furnishings too. They specialise in linens and natural fabrics, with ranges of linens that comprise up to an amazing 54 colours. A large farm table in the centre of the shop serves as a focal point and a generous space to display hand-sewn linen napkins, glassware, pottery, rustic mirrors, soaps and candles. On vintage wood shelves and crates customers will also find numerous beautiful handwoven cottons as well as hand block-printed and indigo-dyed fabrics. The Cloth Shop also stocks lovely floral Indian cotton printed fabrics and crates full of colourful woven trims. All of their fabric stock pairs beautifully with the vintage textiles, blankets and homewares available for sale throughout the shop.

166

COTTON
PRINTS
£6.95 PER METER

If I see a piece of fabric that I adore, I find it very hard to leave it behind. I can always find a bit of space in my forever growing stash!

Melanie Barnes

# BEYOND

One could easily highlight numerous fabric and knitting shops beyond London. London itself is sprawling and rich with fabric, knitting and haberdashery resources among so many other diverse amenities. Parks, restaurants, markets: London truly has a lot to offer across many diverse areas. In this chapter, though, are a few shops any vintage haberdashery lover would be happy to venture to—even on a train journey a couple of hours out of the city. These shops, and in one case a market stall, all centre around time-worn materials that are often pre-loved, perhaps dusty, faded or even chipped or torn—qualities that despite wear reveal past history and character.

Antiques markets are great places to source vintage fabrics and haberdashery, but it's Marina Adinolfi's stall at Sunbury Antiques Market, Kempton Park, that is one of the biggest and best. Further south of London, in East Sussex, The Old Haberdashery has a country cottage atmosphere with a hint of mid-century flair. A bit further south still, in St Leonards-on-Sea is Wayward, a treasure of a haberdashery for anyone who enjoys a good vintage rummage.

33 High Street, Ticehurst
East Sussex TN5 7AS
07891 954971
National Rail: Etchingham
www.theoldhaberdashery.com

# The old Haberdashery

A self-professed "gatherer, accumulator and rescuer of things", Sonia Boriczewski began selling vintage haberdashery at local fairs with the "realisation that at some stage you need to move on and share some of your accumulated vintage wealth". She made her first skirt at the age of seven and she recalls a few of her favourite things to play with during her childhood were her mother's button and sylko thread reels boxes. Another tremendous influence on her and her interest in vintage haberdashery from an early age was her Slovenian grandmother—the village seamstress and a collector with whom Sonia spent every summer during her childhood, enjoying endless hours sifting through the treasure-filled attic.

When Sonia first opened her retail shop in East Sussex it was with an emphasis on vintage homewares and textiles with just a hint of haberdashery. She has since slowly taken her time to research and source materials with a similar ethos and aesthetic to hers, Merchant & Mills being one such company. "The design, the packaging and integrity of their products is something to be admired", Sonia says. Stocking gifts and accessories by local or UK-based makers is also important to Sonia who sells work by designers such as Nancy Nicholson and Judith Brown.

The entire shop—starting with the sight of the front window display— is simply beautiful. Sonia has a genuine gift for merchandising items in her window and throughout the shop in unusual and interesting ways. Whether it's rope dangling through giant wooden quilting hoops, huge branches displayed like a tree adorned with doilies and ornaments, or teacups streaming down from the ceiling on silk ribbons, she transforms her window display seasonally and her shop displays regularly, mixing colours and materials which perfectly complement one another.

SHADE 133

"PERI-LUSTA"
FINE
DARNING THREAD

1930's wallpaper

68 Norman Road
St Leonards-on-Sea
East Sussex TN38 0EJ
07815 013337
National Rail: St Leonards Warrior Square
www.wayward.co

# Wayward

Andrew Hirst has been selling antiques and second-hand treasures since he was 19, but it wasn't until he got his hands on heaps of dead stock ribbon from France that he began to sell vintage haberdashery and fabrics almost exclusively. When he couldn't get rid of the hundreds of rolls of ribbon to one buyer, he took them to his antiques stall at Portobello Road and successfully began selling the ribbon by the metre. Andrew thoroughly enjoyed this new venture and found selling smaller bits of ribbon (as opposed to pricier antiques) took the pressure off customers, creating a more casual interaction between his customers and himself. After building his business at Portobello Road, he opened Wayward in St Leonards-on-Sea in Hastings. The shop's idiosyncratic moniker comes with a story too; "Wayward" is the name Andrew would have given the boat he desperately wanted. When he decided to buy a house and persevere with building his haberdashery business instead, he figured that if he wasn't going to have the boat, he could at least have the name.

Wayward is a beautiful mess in the best way: the decor is haphazard and eccentric; mannequins are draped in ribbons and vintage hats, and trimmings are sprawled about and dripping out of wicker baskets and wood drawers. Collections of materials make dramatic displays such as one large wall of buttons in boxes and another of shimmery metallic thread on wooden reels stacked in a glass case. Despite the random nature of the shop's styling, Andrew's stock is of the highest quality. Having come from a family of tailors, Andrew seems to have an innate sense for sourcing exceptional materials. One could spend hours admiring his brilliant selection of fabrics and vintage haberdashery.

177

Kempton Park Race Course
Staines Road East
Sunbury-on-Thames
Middlesex TW16 5AQ
01932 230946
www.sunburyantiques.com
min_adinolfi@yahoo.com

# Marina Adinolfi

Raised by a stylish Italian mother who was skilled in both making and modifying her clothes, Marina Adinolfi grew up with an understanding and appreciation for colour and fabrics. Though she had very few dresses, her mother always emphasised the quality of the fabrics and how garments were made, noticing small details in areas such as the stitching and seams. While Marina says she didn't inherit her mother's gift for dressing so well, she did inherit her interest in all manner of sewing materials—beautiful fabrics, threads and buttons, among others.

Marina has a stall at Kempton Antiques Fair, Ardingly Antiques Fair, Malvern flea market, the boot sale at Chiswick in London, and at Newark, Shepton Mallet. Being as much of a collector of old photographs, postcards, paintings, shells and bird's nests as she is of textiles and sewing paraphernalia, Marina's market stalls always look like artful table displays, with items, though dissimilar in nature, arranged by groupings of similar colours.

Marina's customers range from those looking for goods to stock in their boutiques, or those looking to use the items in dressmaking or crafts, to those who simply like the items as decorative pieces, and her vintage dress patterns, buttons, thread, fabric remnants, clothing and hats are all very popular with customers who appreciate a bit of history in the materials they buy.

181

Some of my favourite moments in sewing are when I pull out a vintage fabric or trim that I've collected at a flea market or estate sale, and it is the perfect fit for my project. I love the idea that someone owned these things before me, and that we have a shared interest and source of delight.

Melody Miller

**XX**n addition to shops included in the guide, many of which offer shopping online, here is a list of additional online shopping resources in the UK for fabric, knitting and haberdashery supplies, as well as a list of inspirational bloggers and notable craft fairs and events.

## Shopping Online

### Abakhan
www.abakhan.co.uk
Abakhan is a fabric, yarn and craft supply online retailer that sells reasonably priced supplies.

### Bedecked
www.bedecked.co.uk
Bedecked's emphasis is on haberdashery, providing buttons, beads, ribbon and trimmings.

### Betty & Peggy Haberdashery
www.bettyandpeggyhaberdashery.co.uk
Betty & Peggy carries a selection of buttons, trimmings and other essentials for sewing and crafting such as purse making accessories as well as a selection of vintage haberdashery.

### Beyond Fabrics
www.beyond-fabrics.co.uk
Beyond Fabrics is an online retailer that sells patchwork and quilting fabrics, craft supplies as well as sewing and quilting kits.

### Black Sheep Wools
www.blacksheepwools.com
Black Sheep Wools sells yarn and supplies for knitting, crochet and needlework as well as a range of fabrics, patterns and books.

### Croft Mill
www.croftmill.co.uk
Croft Mill specialises in fabrics, including a number of speciality fabrics such as waterproof and outdoor fabrics.

### Deramores
www.deramores.com
Deramores is an online retailer selling yarn and supplies for knitting and crochet as well as patterns, books and craft supplies.

### Ditto Fabrics
www.dittofabrics.co.uk
Ditto, a fabric shop in Brighton, sells many of their dressmaking and craft fabrics online.

### Donna Flower
www.donnaflower.com
Donna Flower specialises in vintage and antique fabrics, ranging from the nineteenth century to the 1980s as well as vintage haberdashery and housewares.

### Dragonfly Fabrics
www.dragonflyfabrics.co.uk
Dragonfly Fabrics sells a range of dressmaking fabrics, haberdashery and patterns.

### Efabrics
www.efabrics.co.uk
Efabrics offers a large selection of inexpensive fabrics and haberdashery items.

### Elephant in My Handbag
www.elephantinmyhandbag.com
Elephant in My Handbag sells a large selection of fabrics for quilting and patchwork, including many children's and novelty prints.

### Fabric Godmother
www.fabricgodmother.co.uk
Fabric Godmother sells designer fabrics, haberdashery, kits and patterns.

### Fabric HQ
www.fabrichq.co.uk
Fabric HQ carries a range of dressmaking and patchwork fabrics and has a sewing studio in Buckinghamshire.

### Fancy Moon
www.fancymoon.co.uk
Fancy Moon offer bold, modern furnishing, dressmaking and quilting fabrics and a selection of patterns from contemporary designers.

### Fondant Fabrics
www.fondantfabrics.co.uk
Fondant Fabrics have a range of dressmaking fabrics and sewing patterns.

### Guthrie & Ghani
www.guthrie-ghani.co.uk
Guthrie & Ghani sell fabrics, yarn and haberdashery supplies. Former Great British Sewing Bee finalist, Lauren Guthrie, owns this Birmingham based shop. In addition to the online store, her blog offers sewing tutorials and tips.

### Hobbycraft
www.hobbycraft.co.uk
Hobbycraft is a general craft superstore with individual sections for fabric, knitting and haberdashery as well as equipment, such as sewing machines.

Jaycotts
www.jaycotts.co.uk
Jaycotts sells a huge range of haberdashery supplies, equipment and sewing patterns.

JosyRose
www.josyrose.com
JosyRose is a haberdashery with a large selection of craft supplies, trimmings and jewellery supplies.

Kettle Yarn Co
www.kettleyarnco.co.uk
Kettle Yarn Co specialises in hand-dyed, low pill wearable yarns. The Kettle Yarn Co blog is filled with inspiring photos of knitwear made using their yarns.

Kitschy Coo
www.kitschycoo.bigcartel.com
Kitschy Coo sells fun, whimsical fabrics designed primarily for childrenswear. Their blog features tutorials and sewing tips and also includes an extensive list of online fabric shop retailers.

Knitshop.co.uk
www.knitshop.co.uk
Knitshop.co.uk offers a range of knitting and felting supplies.

Lady Sew and Sew
www.ladysewandsew.co.uk
Lady Sew and Sew sells designer fabrics for patchwork, dressmaking and general crafts as well as yarn, patterns and books.

M is for Make
www.misformake.co.uk
M is for Make is an online fabric and haberdashery shop that stocks a large selection of prints from contemporary designers.

Meadow Yarn
www.meadowyarn.co.uk
Meadow Yarn sells a variety of yarn and a selection of patterns, books and magazines for knitting and crochet.

Minerva Crafts
www.minervacrafts.com
Minerva Crafts offers an enormous selection of fabric, quilting materials, needlework supplies, and yarn.

Mrs Moon
www.mrsmoon.co.uk
Mrs Moon is an online shop that offers a range of knitting supplies and haberdashery.

My Fabric House
www.myfabrichouse.co.uk
My Fabric House specialises in cotton and linen fabrics in children's and novelty prints along with various haberdashery.

Myfabrics.co.uk
www.myfabrics.co.uk
My Fabrics sells a range of fabrics and sewing supplies at reasonable prices.

Plush Addict
www.plushaddict.co.uk
Plush Addict stocks a large selection of fabrics for dressmaking, patchwork, crafts and housewares.

Overspill
www.etsy.com/uk/shop/Overspill
Overspill is an Etsy haberdashery store that sells a variety of buttons and trimmings.

Remnant Kings
www.remnantkings.co.uk
Remnant Kings sells a range of fabrics for dressmaking, patchwork and housewares as well as haberdashery.

Seamstar
www.seamstar.co.uk
Seamstar carries a range fabric and haberdashery and often has fabrics offered at a discount.

Sew Essential
www.sewessential.co.uk
Sew Essential provides a large selection of fabric, patterns, specialised haberdashery, equipment and various crafting supplies.

Sewbox
www.sewbox.co.uk
Sew Box specialises in selling cotton and Liberty fabrics and patterns by contemporary designers.

Sewing Online
www.sewing-online.com
Sewing Online has a large selection of patchwork and quilting fabrics, craft supplies as well as sewing patterns and general haberdashery.

Sherwoods Online Fabric Store
www.sherwoodsfabrics.co.uk
Sherwoods carries a variety of fabrics and haberdashery and sells a large selection of remnants and remnant sacks.

Simply Sewing
www.simplysewing.co.uk
Simply Sewing is a haberdashery store that sells items ranging from buttons and sequins to elastics, ribbons, and feathers.

Stitch Organics
www.etsy.com/uk/shop/stitchorganics
Stitch Organics sells all organic products and has a selection of fabrics and haberdashery.

Tangled Yarn
www.tangled-yarn.co.uk
Tangled Yarn offers materials, patterns and tools for knitting and crochet.

Teasleweeds
www.etsy.com/uk/shop/Teasleweeds
Teasleweeds is an Etsy store that sells vintage haberdashery and housewares.

The Cotton Patch
www.cottonpatch.co.uk
The Cotton Patch sells a variety of fabrics and sewing tools, with a focus on quilting supplies.

The Little Button Shop
www.thelittlebuttonshop.co.uk
The Little Button Shop sells sewing and crafting supplies.

The Magpie Haberdashery
www.etsy.com/uk/shop/magpiehaberdashery
The Magpie Haberdashery is an Etsy shop that sells ribbon, trim, buttons and beads.

The Makery
www.themakery.co.uk
The Makery offers fabric, haberdashery and kits, and hosts workshops both at their shop in Bath and at the John Lewis London Oxford Street location.

Traynor's Trimmings
www.traynorstrimmings.co.uk
Traynor's Trimmings has a store location in London as well as selling trimmings and haberdashery through their online store.

Vintage Pattern Collective
www.vintagepatterncollective.net
The Vintage Pattern Collective is a tremendous resource for anyone interested in vintage sewing patterns. The website links to numerous vintage pattern sellers on Etsy. Though many are based in the US, most offer worldwide shipping.

Inspiring Blogs

Apartment Apothecary
www.apartmentapothecary.com
Stylist Katie Orme writes posts on inspiring interiors and craft projects for the home.

Almond Rock
www.almondrock.co.uk
Sewist Amy writes about her latest dressmaking projects.

Champagne and Qiviut
www.champagneandqiviut.com
Knitter Allison posts about her various knitting projects and other projects such as her podcast Yarn In the City in conjunction with friend Rachel of Porpoise Knits.

Comfortstitching
www.comfortstitching.typepad.co.uk
Fabric designer and author Aneela Hoey posts about her various craft projects including quilting and embroidery.

Curious Handmade
www.curioushandmade.com
Knitter and pattern designer Helen Stewart writes about her knitting projects and her popular knitting patterns and podcast.

Diary of a Chain Stitcher
www.chainstitcher.blogspot.com
Sewist Fiona posts about her dressmaking projects and writes in depth reviews of independent sewing patterns.

Did You Make That?
www.didyoumakethat.com
Sewist Karen documents her dressmaking and knitting projects.

Dock + Nettle
www.dock-and-nettle.blogspot.co.uk
Maker Rachelle Blondel writes about sustainable and simple living and documents her sewing, knitting and crochet projects.

**Emma Varnam**
www.emmavarnam.co.uk
Emma Varnam is a crafty mother who knits and crochets and offers free patterns and tutorials on her blog.

**Feeling Stitchy**
www.feelingstitchy.com
Feeling Stitchy is an embroidery blog collective with multiple contributors who write about embroidery as well as other stitching related topics.

**Geoffrey & Grace**
www.geoffreyandgrace.com
Maker Melanie Barnes writes about her vintage inspired sewing projects.

**Jessie Chorley Inspirations**
www.jessiechorleyinspirations.com
Textile and embroidery artist Jessie Chorley posts images of her stitched works and her adventures teaching embroidery workshops in the UK and Europe.

**Junkaholique**
www.junkaholique.com
Jewellery designer and sewist Artemis Russell writes about her jewellerymaking, sewing projects and outings with her family.

**Knitted Bliss**
www.knittedbliss.com
Knitter Julie writes posts about her sewing and knitting projects and provides tutorials and patterns.

**Mollie Makes**
www.molliemakes.com
The team behind popular UK craft magazine *Mollie Makes* write posts about upcoming craft events, interviews with designer-makers and they offer patterns, printables and tutorials.

**My Oh Sew Vintage Life**
www.vintageinkfairy.blogspot.co.uk
Sewist Emmie documents her sewing projects, many of which are based on vintage patterns or inspired by 1940s and 1950s fashion.

**Patchwork Harmony**
www.patchworkharmony.co.uk
Writer Caroline Rowland offers DIY tutorials for small projects for the home, documents her craft projects and writes posts on beautiful interiors.

**Permanent Style**
www.permanentstyle.co.uk
Launched in 2007 by journalist and editor Simon Crompton, Permanent Style is the go-to place for information on men's luxury tailoring.

**Porpoise Knits**
www.porpoiseknits.com
Rachel writes about her knitting and sells knitting patterns as well as her own hand-dyed fibre Porpoise Fur. She also hosts the Yarn in the City podcast with friend Allison of Champagne and Qiviut.

**Posie Gets Cozy**
www.posiegetscozy.com
Devoted crafter Alicia Paulson writes inspiring posts about her embroidery, sewing, knitting and crochet projects as well as recipes, family outings and her life in general.

**PutYourFlareOn**
www.putyourflareon.blogs.com
Knitter Aimee Gille writes about her knitting projects, her family and her wonderful Paris knitting shops.

**Sew Over It Blog**
www.sewoverit.co.uk/blog/
Lisa Comfort, owner of the Sew Over It sewing lounges in London, shares her latest projects with readers, provides tips and "sewalongs" and keeps readers updated on current events at the shops.

**So Zo…What Do You Know?**
www.sozowhatdoyouknow.blogspot.co.uk/
Sewing teacher and pattern designer Zoe offers tips and tutorials on dressmaking and refashioning your wardrobe.

**The Brodwick Design Studio**
www.thebrodwickdesignstudio.blogspot.co.uk
Product designer, digital pattern cutter and sewist Rachel Walker posts weekly updates on craft events, new pattern releases and what London bloggers are sewing. She also has helpful city guides featuring fabric, knitting and haberdashery shops throughout London.

**The Craft Sessions**
www.craftsessions.com
Sewist and knitter Felicia Semple writes posts about her sewing projects and musings about crafting as well as featuring bloggers' makes from around the world in her "I Made This" feature.

The Thrifty Stitcher
www.thethriftystitcher.co.uk/blog
Author and sewing teacher Claire-Louise
Hardie posts sewing tips and tutorials on
her blog.

Tilly and The Buttons
www.tillyandthebuttons.com
Author and pattern designer Tilly Walnes
writes posts about her latest sewing
patterns, current sewing projects, and
offers sewing tips and tutorials.

What Katie Sews
www.whatkatiesews.net
Sewist Katie documents her progress
in making a wearable wardrobe for
everyday clothes.

Yarnstorm Press
www.yarnstormpress.co.uk
Author Jane Brocket writes about
art, literature, markets, sewing, knitting,
crochet and her self-published
city guides.

Craft Fairs and Craft Events

Country Living Fair
www.countrylivingfair.com
The Country Living Fair showcases work
from individual crafters, interior designers
and antiques and vintage dealers.

Crafters4Crafters Exhibition
www.craft4crafters.co.uk
The Crafters4Crafters Exhibition features
numerous crafters and offers a range
of different events including lectures,
demonstrations and workshops.

Crafty Fox Market
www.craftyfoxmarket.co.uk
Crafty Fox market features indie
designers' handmade wares.

I Knit Fandango
www.iknit.org.uk/iknitfandango.html
I Knit Fandango is a yarn festival
featuring a large selection of independent
yarn makers.

The Handmade Fair
www.thehandmadefair.com
The Handmade Fair is a craft fair and
event for short workshops in knitting,
stitching and papercrafts.

Made London
www.madelondon.org
Made London is a craft fair that
showcases the work of innovative
designers and makers.

Renegade Craft Fair
www.renegadecraft.com/london
Renegade Craft Fair features
independent designers' clothing,
housewares and accessories.

Selvedge Fair
http://www.selvedge.org
Selvedge Fair features work by
textile, embroidery, jewellery and
homeware designers.

Textile Forum
www.textileforum.org.uk
Textile Forum is a bi-annual textile show
showcasing fabrics from numerous
designers for dressmaking, tailoring, and
general crafting.

The Decorative Living Fair
www.carolinezoob.co.uk
The Decorative Fair showcases a wide
range of vintage household goods and
craft products in beautiful settings.

The Knitting & Stitching Show
www.theknittingandstitchingshow.com
The Knitting & Stitching Show is
a textile and fibre fair featuring
numerous companies that sell products
for sewing, knitting, embroidery and
general crafts as well as hosting a
variety of craft workshops.

The Stitching, Sewing and Hobbycrafts Show
www.stitchandhobby.co.uk
The Stitching, Sewing and Hobbycrafts
Show presents various products for
sewing, knitting and hobbycrafts and
includes workshops.

Yarn in the City
www.yarninthecity.com/pop-up-marketplace
The Yarn in the City Pop-Up Marketplace
hosts dyers and designers selling a varied
selection of yarn, accessories and tools
for fibre crafts.

**L**eigh Metcalf is an avid crafter, freelance writer and photographer, specialising in documenting character-filled interiors and handmade products. Originally from the US, she now lives in South London with her wonderful husband and two lively daughters. She enjoys posting about craft projects, travels, food and her adventures in London on her blog Found, Now Home. Her work has appeared in magazines such as *Mollie Makes* and *Pretty Nostalgic*.

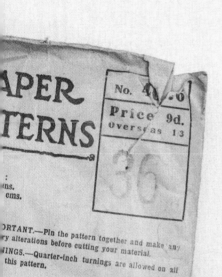

hank you to Black Dog Publishing for giving me the opportunity to write this book—a dream come true—and to Ana Teodoro and Leanne Hayman in particular for all the time and effort they put into bringing it to life. Thanks to all the shop owners for letting me photograph their beautiful shops and for providing me with helpful information and to Ryn Frank for her charming illustrations. Many thanks to Alicia Paulson, Melody Miller, Jane Brocket, Melanie Barnes, Aimée Gille, Jessie Chorley and Rachelle Blondel for contributing their lovely thoughts on what craft supplies mean to them. For lending me so many pretty sewing and knitting bits and bobs, thank you Emmeline Wilson, Katie Evans and Pascale Spall. To Laura Jarvis, Lisa Wilson, Caroline Rowland, Lara Watson, Lisa Comfort, Lauren Smith and Stephen Dobranski who have all in their own way led me on the path to this book in one way or another, I can't thank you enough. And I'm forever grateful for the love and support from my wonderful family: Mom, Page, Andrew, Lois and Ellie.

Black Dog Publishing Limited
10a Acton Street, London WC1X 9NG
United Kingdom

t. +44 (0)207 713 5097
f. +44 (0)207 713 8682
info@blackdogonline.com
www.blackdogonline.com

All opinions expressed within this publication are those
of the authors and not necessarily of the publisher.

Designed by Ana Teodoro at Black Dog Publishing.
Illustrations by Ryn Frank.
All photography by Leigh Metcalf except for
p 37 (top right) courtesy of Cloth House
and pp 90–91 courtesy of Aimée Gille.

British Library Cataloguing-in-Publication Data.
A CIP record for this book is available from the British Library.

ISBN 978 1 910433 52 2

Black Dog Publishing is an environmentally responsible company.
*London Stitch and Knit* is printed on sustainably sourced paper.

art design fashion
history photography
theory and things

black dog
publishing

www.blackdogonline.com

london uk